N𝒲P

National *Writing* Project

Teachers at the Center

Teachers at the Center

A Memoir
of the Early Years
of the National Writing Project

JAMES GRAY

National *Writing* **Project**

Berkeley, California

NATIONAL WRITING PROJECT, BERKELEY 94720

Please direct reprinting requests and book orders to:
National Writing Project
2105 Bancroft Way #1042
Berkeley, CA 94720-1042

Telephone: 510-642-0963
Fax: 510-642-4545

Editor: Art Peterson
Production Editors: Roxanne Barber, Rebekah Truemper, and Barbara Yoder
Design and Layout: Judy Anderson
Cover Design: Judy Anderson
Copyeditor: Jeff Campbell
Proofreader: M. Kate St. Clair

Library of Congress Cataloging-in-Publication Data

Gray, James, 1927-
    Teachers at the center: a memoir of the early years of the National
Writing Project / James Gray.
        p. cm.
    ISBN 1-883920-16-7 (pbk.)
    1. English teachers—Training of—California—Berkeley. 2. English
language—Rhetoric—Study and teaching—California—Berkeley. 3. Report
writing—Study and teaching (Higher)—California—Berkeley. 4. National
Writing Project (U.S.) I. Title.
PE1405.U6 G73 2000
428'.0071'179467—dc21

                                                00-049019

This book is dedicated to

*the thousands of classroom teachers in
our nation's schools who have participated in writing
project programs over the past twenty-six years*

~

*the local university site directors, current and past,
whose embracing of the Bay Area Writing Project
model made the National Writing Project possible*

~

Roderic Park, our first and greatest champion

Contents

Foreward

At a national conference in San Francisco in 1977, I had a life-changing experience. My colleagues John Brereton and Sondra Perl and I were at the Conference on College Composition and Communication to present our research findings drawn from a project we had been conducting while we were faculty members at three different branches of the City University of New York (CUNY). We had been investigating how CUNY freshmen, admitted under the open admissions program, became proficient writers. At the conclusion of our session, Jim Gray, director of the Bay Area Writing Project, and Mary K. Healy, the project's codirector, approached us and asked a simple question. "Would you folks like to start a writing project?"

At the time, we had no idea what a "writing project" was. We also knew little of schools and of teachers in public schools. Yet, for reasons that I am unsure of even to this day, we said yes to Jim's offer. A few months later, in the summer of 1978, the first invitational institute of the New York City Writing Project was underway.

Perhaps the reason John, Sondra, and I felt connected with Jim and his colleagues in their still-fledgling endeavor was the belief we shared with them that most professional educators, and indeed the public at large, failed to recognize the impact that writing has on learning. Our experience teaching freshmen at CUNY raised an interesting question. What are the schools doing (or not doing) that leads to our students' inability to write well?

Many of our students appeared to have had little or no opportunities to write extensively in or out of school. Those teachers who did care about teaching writing had developed strategies in isolation from their colleagues, creating their own theory of action, finding their way by trial and error. And no one asked these teachers to share their hard-won knowledge.

It was Jim Gray's vision to turn the body of knowledge and expertise that existed in classrooms everywhere into a model for professional development. Teachers knew things that people on the other side of the classroom door did not. So why not ask teachers to share their knowledge? Shouldn't expert teachers be among the teachers of teachers? It seemed obvious to Jim that a skilled and knowledgeable demonstration by a classroom teacher would be believable to other teachers in a way that a performance by an outside consultant would never be.

Teachers at the Center is Jim's account of how the concept of teachers teaching teachers, and other key writing project ideas, evolved. Even though these ideas have been refined over the years, and even though the writing project has expanded beyond its original boundaries, the writing project model remains much as it was explained to us back in 1978. Every summer at National Writing Project sites throughout the country, writing teachers at all grade levels are invited to institutes where they demonstrate for one another approaches to teaching writing that they've used successfully in their classrooms. In addition, the teachers write and share their writing in response groups. Finally, they read, discuss, and write about research and important works in the literature of writing education.

Having developed a sense of their own authority and expertise through this experience, these teachers then conduct school-year inservice programs that disseminate and honor their knowledge. Many also take on leadership responsibilities in their schools and in the larger educational community.

From the beginning, Jim Gray knew he was on to something. He never had any doubts that the writing project model would succeed. One wonders, though, if he understood just how successful it would be. The project that began in 1974 with one site at the University of California, Berkeley has grown to 168 sites at colleges and universities in forty-nine states. Years before I arrived to assume, on Jim's retirement, the position of NWP executive director, the federal government had recognized the writing project's important work and provided us with funding, and this funding has increased steadily.

Teachers at the Center is the story of how our model came into being. Underlying this tale is the attitude that has made the writing project possible: Jim's respect for teachers. In the course of his career, he has worked with countless teachers, and almost without exception, he has instilled in them new confidence in their special knowledge about the importance of their work and the belief that they can make a difference in their classrooms and beyond. One reason Jim has had this effect on teachers is that the writing project model he developed does not dictate "The One Right Way to Teach." His view of varying classroom strategies and curricula is ecumenical. The question he most often asks teachers is one we might also ask heart surgeons, highway engineers, or members of any other profession. When you reflect on your practice, how can you explain why you do what you do?

Jim believes that teachers need the freedom to find practices that work in their classrooms, but that they must also accept the responsibility for rationalizing these practices. He knows too, however, that this is a stance that takes time and experience, and he respects those who are still struggling with their practice. Central to Jim's work is the key idea that teachers must be honored for their commitment, knowledge, and creativity. In this regard, and in many other ways, the National Writing Project is dedicated to continuing Jim Gray's legacy.

RICHARD STERLING
Executive Director, National Writing Project

Acknowledgments

I want to acknowledge my indebtedness to Leo Ruth, Peter Newmeyer, and Joye Alberts for their insightful suggestions; to Keith Tandy for telling me of the happy memories reading the book brought back to him; to Mary Ann Smith, Jane Juska, and Don Gallehr for the hours they spent with my writing, making helpful if sometimes blunt comments; to Miles Myers, who corrected my memory of events during the early years of the project; to my wife, Stephanie, for her helpful editing and for her understanding throughout the long time it took me to write this book; and to Art Peterson for getting me back to writing with his suggestion: "Why don't you tell stories? You're a good storyteller. Tell stories."

Chapter One

EARLY INFLUENCES

IN 1943, ON THE FIRST DAY OF MY JUNIOR YEAR at Whitefish Bay High School in Milwaukee, Wisconsin, I was sitting in the last row in my trigonometry class waiting for class to begin when Miss Popham, a slight, dark-haired woman of indeterminate age and one of my former English teachers, walked into the room, came over to me, and asked me to come out into the hall. "I want you to join my new class on the English novel," she said. In fact, the class was meeting across the hall at that very moment. I followed her, and when she opened the door, I found myself with a group of about nine or ten other students—juniors and seniors, all boys—who probably had been led out of their classes that morning also. I never stepped back into trigonometry.

Miss Popham's class, though I would never have guessed it at the time, led to my becoming an English teacher and influenced my understanding of teachers and teaching. It provided me with a model to work toward in my early teaching years. The plan of the class was simple. She presented us with a twenty-five-page syllabus of "Readings for the English Novel Course," a listing of authors and recommended traditional English novels. We then were free to pick whatever novels we wanted to read throughout the semester. I remember that one of my close friends in the class read the first six of John Galsworthy's Forsyte novels. It was up to us to find the books. As a result, I spent much time in the school library, the local village library, the large Milwaukee public library, and in the local and downtown bookstores, sometimes buying one of the new paperback books, which had just begun to appear.

Each day, except Friday, we read in class while Miss Popham toured the room, sitting down in a desk next to each of us and talking to us individually about the book we were reading and how we were getting on. Fridays were special days. One of us would talk to the class about the novel he was reading, and Miss Popham would get us all talking together about the other books we were reading. That was it, one novel every week or two for the rest of the semester. More than fifty years later, I still have sharp memories of Miss Popham. I enjoyed having her talk to me when she was making her rounds—brief little book talks that were just for me. I have memories just as sharp about spending time in the libraries and bookstores, sitting on the floor facing the shelves of books, a lap full of books, edging myself one way or the other to look at more titles, walking up and down the aisles, week after week, looking for the books on our list. I remember the unique smell of the books and their traditional library bindings in green, tan, blue, and red with white ink printing. I had been reading widely—if you count the Hardy Boys and the X-Bar-X Boys and *The Shadow* magazine—since about fifth or sixth grade, but I became a serious and enthusiastic reader that year at Whitefish Bay High School.

Now, looking back, I understand how my experience of Miss Popham's class influenced my views of education and teaching. I had thrived in Miss Popham's class because she was in charge of her own curriculum. She had a wonderful idea and freedom to teach as she wished. I still think hers is the best way to organize a literature class in high school if the goal is to encourage wide reading and the love of books. My own best teaching in high school reflected my attempt to replicate the spirit of that 1943 class.

⤳ The Right Place, the Right Time ⤳

TWO YEARS AFTER LEAVING MISS POPHAM, I entered the University of Wisconsin at Madison, on the shores of Lake Mendota. *Life* magazine once described Madison as "the most beautiful small town in the country." I had come to the university from a lower-middle-class background. My father was a salesman for Hershey chocolate during the Depression years, when people couldn't afford to buy chocolate, and during the war years, when the product was largely unavailable. Although my mother had been a teacher, my parents had little education in any of the subjects I was to study at the university, but they had faith in me. Because they had no money to support a child in college, I earned my room and board by working ten hours every day of the week during the summer at the Pabst Brewing Company in Milwaukee. For the next five years, the university was to become my oasis.

Here I carved out for myself a traditional classical education by majoring in comparative literature and by choosing additional courses such as Greek and French language classes, English, ancient, medieval, and modern philosophy, as well as several classes in the history of art and music. I spent five years reading the great books of the world. It was a disciplined foundation that has given me confidence throughout my teaching career.

The years 1945 to 1951 were a time of change for the country. I saw the end of World War II and the beginnings of the Cold War. By the time I was a sophomore, the campus was swarming with veterans on the G.I. Bill of Rights. It was a time that generated a string of new delights—such as foreign films from Italy, France, Russia, and England unlike any I had seen before. I met a friend every Friday afternoon in the Frank Lloyd Wright little theater to see our foreign film of the week. The first long-playing records began showing up in the stores, and I listened to music that I had never heard before by composers familiar and unfamiliar. It was a renaissance. State Street, with the university at one end and the state capitol at the other, had scores of college shops and used and new bookstores, which were stocking increasing numbers of new and unheard-of paperbacks from equally new publishers. The Bratt House, a restaurant with its little patio in the back, was mobbed every night. There were ice cream parlors, one per block it seemed, where we could buy hot fudge sundaes made with creamy milk chocolate, and there were great Italian restaurants for our Friday night, male-only, spaghetti-and-meatball dinners after the enforced 10:00 P.M. curfew for girls. Lake Mendota was a dominant presence. On balmy summer evenings, I would walk along the heavily wooded path that followed the shoreline from the dorms to the student union on my way to meet my growing number of friends. On weekends, we would sit for hours talking about books and courses and professors on the wide terrace that extends from the student union's Rathskeller to the water. My happy memories of Madison are endless. The Pro Arte Quartet was in permanent residence. I would go to the union frequently just to buy one or two of the huge chocolate doughnuts made out of bread dough, not cake dough, a long-gone culinary art. For minimal cost, I purchased sets of coupon books good for the whole year for every athletic event, every play, every ballet, and every concert, many of which were presented in the new and exciting Frank Lloyd Wright theater. I saw my first ballet in that theater, and I heard my first symphony concert there—the San Francisco Symphony under the direction of Pierre Monteux playing Cesar Franck's Symphony in D minor—one of my favorites ever since.

As the Cold War developed in the early 1950s, Wisconsin's senator and demagogic anticommunist, Joe McCarthy, began making national headlines. The university and Madison, however, formed a liberal oasis in the state—as they still do. Madison's major newspaper was the *Capital Times,* one of the great liberal papers in the nation. Madison was home to Robert M. La Follette, founder of the Progressive Party, and it is still the editorial home of *The Progressive.* With the university's famous 1894 Board of Regents commitment to freedom and truth, the University of Wisconsin had no need for a Berkeley-style Free Speech Movement.

> *Whatever may be the limitations which trammel inquiry elsewhere, we believe that the great state university of Wisconsin should ever encourage that sifting and winnowing by which alone the truth can be found.*

There were two student communist clubs approved on campus, and friends and I would go to the meetings on occasion, initially just to see what a communist looked like, but also as part of our growing political awareness and involvement. I left a sentimental Republican tradition in my family, which frequently teared up at the very thought of the Grand Old Party, and became a Democrat, working and voting for Harry Truman in 1948. During his famous whistle-stop campaign, Truman came to the campus, and I sat on the stage about five feet behind him as he gave his talk. There was an overflow audience that night in the great stone and half-timbered agricultural show barn.

~

As a comparative literature major at Madison, I was to fall again under the influence of another dynamic educator, Philo Buck, the chairman and founder of the department, which was the nation's first in comparative literature. He was a tall, white-haired man with a wonderful soft and hypnotic voice. He was the most inspirational teacher I have ever had, a magical storyteller who introduced the great books of the world to his students with story after story about authors and books of other times and places. I was totally swayed by him, and I wasn't alone. A student once turned to me on the first day of one of his classes and said, "I'd take a course from Buck even if it were taught in Chinese!" His classes were large, and many were broadcast over the university's radio station WHA to listeners throughout the state. In one memorable year-long drama class, tragedy in the fall and comedy in the spring, Buck lectured on Monday and Wednesday about the play we were reading that week, telling related stories about the author and his time, and on Friday we would meet in the WHA studio theater to listen as radio actors performed a one-hour radio version of the play we had just read.

Buck operated at a level that was all his own. To personalize great literature for us, he constantly drew on his own unique background. He had been born in India into a home of British missionaries. He was raised bilingual in English and Hindi and had a remarkable gift for languages. It seemed that every book he taught, ancient or modern, he had read in the original. As he lectured on a particular author or a particular work, he always had some personal story to tell us. "I was in the south of France when I first saw Rostand's *Cyrano de Bergerac*, and I knew I just had to meet the author, so I went to Paris and . . ." We were transfixed. When we were reading Montaigne's *Essays*, he described the ancient tower that Montaigne lived in and told us about reading the aphorisms Montaigne had carved into the tower's huge timbers. When he was commenting on the remarkable acoustics of ancient Greek theaters, he told of his experiment to test whether they were still as acoustically perfect today. He asked his wife to sit in the rising stands, while he stood on the stage reciting a passage from a Greek play in his natural voice, and then, still speaking in the same voice, asking his wife if she could hear him clearly. She nodded yes. He brought us into his world. One time, India's prime minister, Pandit Nehru, on a trip to Washington, made a special trip to Madison to see his old friend Philo Buck, and Buck had his friend speak to several hundred of us from a balcony on the student union as we stood on the terrace.

In my later career, when I would enter a classroom as a supervisor of student teachers, I would sometimes not be able to find the teacher. Eventually, a student would direct me to a rug where the teacher was energetically engaged in a writing response group or a discussion of a story. Generally, I've admired this practice, as it embodies the ideal of the teacher as a facilitator of learning. But I always remember that this bias of mine needs to take into account the Philo Bucks of this world, the teacher who by dint of his or her personality inspires a lifelong passion for learning, as Buck did for me. One of the tenets of the writing project has become "There is no right way to teach writing." When I think about Philo Buck and Miss Popham in tandem, I understand there is no one right way to teach.

⤙ *The Real World Encroaches* ⤚

I STAYED ON FOR A FIFTH YEAR AT MADISON to get an M.A. I had loved the first four years so much that I wanted to enjoy the world of the student for as long as I could. I started a campus literary magazine at that time and moved into an apartment on the lake with the editor of the campus humor magazine. I had not thought of a career—at least not in the way most of my friends had. I was thinking only of taking more and more courses and of reading more and more books and, in the vaguest way, of probably eventually getting a Ph.D. Work was not part of my agenda. However, by the time I was studying for my master's degree, Philo Buck had retired, and I found that working under the new chairman of the comparative literature department, Professor Orsini, recently from Florence, was quite a different matter. The world of reading the great books that I had so loved had evolved into a world of scholarship, which I did not love at all. So, after receiving my M.A. with permission to move into the Ph.D. program, I left that wonderful university for good.

During my years at Madison, I had never considered a teaching career, certainly not a career in writing education, partly because writing—student writing—was not a priority, even for my most excellent instructors. We took our essay test, did "reports" on authors and books, and researched term papers that demonstrated our ability to collect and organize facts. But we never received help from our professors with ways we might establish a personal voice, experiment with sentence forms, or revise to clarify our ideas. Since this was the pedagogy I knew, I did not criticize it. Whatever needs I had for more expressive outlets were met when I founded the campus literary magazine.

I think what happened next has happened in a general way to many liberal arts graduates who eventually became teachers. I tried to find a job. Looking in the want-ad section of the newspaper, I didn't find a fit. I didn't qualify for anything, although personnel directors insisted I was overqualified. To help me out, a college friend who worked in the personnel department of a large battery factory hired me. I was assigned to a huge "wet room" where new batteries, one after another, came out of an opening in a wall. It was my job to dry them, using a small compressed-air hose, before they went back behind the wall through another hole. The openings were so high that I had to stand, the wet batteries came out of the first hole so fast that I had to pay constant attention to what I was doing, and the air hose was so short that I could never look around and had only the batteries and the wall and the two openings to look at. I lasted one day.

Next I found a job working in a run-down warehouse for an interesting old man who preferred opera to business, which was why he soon went bankrupt. I didn't have much to do except look after the furniture that was left over from his previous office furniture store, so I read much of each day, snuggled close to an old pot-bellied stove. My boss had a pure high tenor voice, and when he was around, he frequently entertained me by singing the songs of John McCormack, a famous Irish tenor of the twenties and thirties. It was sad to see such a sweet man go under. When everything that could be sold was sold, I moved on to a white-collar job in a large Milwaukee manufacturing plant, where I read blueprints to determine how many of what parts would need to be ordered for different jobs. I sat at a desk in a large office room along with fifty or sixty others all doing the same kind of work. It was the type of dronelike office scene that was often satirized in the films of the 1950s and 1960s. My boss—another kind man who raised English bulldogs and spent much of his time talking to me about his dogs and about his constant search for his next used but perfect Cadillac—sat right behind me and looked after me. It was clear to him that I knew nothing about blueprints. I was hired, I believe, because I once had a job inking over penciled lines on army maps during World War II. But understanding a blueprint with the exactness required was not easy. I made frequent mistakes during my training period, and when I was on my own, I misread one blueprint in a major way, ordering two thousand parts instead of the two hundred called for. My boss took me aside and suggested that there might be other lines of work that I would find closer to my interests.

My next job was one that brought me closer to my life's work. I went to work for a Milwaukee Social Center, that wonderful socialist idea that in the evening turned many of Milwaukee's public schools into community centers for the use and enjoyment of neighborhood families. I showed old movies, supervised tango classes, and did some janitorial work. I had a good time on the job, but I knew I was spinning my wheels. And then my aunt and uncle in California presented me with an idea that had never occurred to me: Why not become a teacher? They were both teachers, my mother had been a teacher, and my grandfather had started out as a teacher. The more I thought about the idea, the more I liked it. So I enrolled as soon as I could in the teacher education department at Wisconsin State University, now the University of Wisconsin, Milwaukee, and previously Milwaukee Normal, where my mother had received her credential as well.

Chapter Two

BEGINNING TEACHER AND BEYOND

∽ *The Worst and Best of Teacher Education* ∽

THE TEACHING PROGRAM AT WISCONSIN STATE was both something to wonder at and something wonderful. I wondered, for instance, at the teacher who taught the English methods class, certainly a key class for someone like me who wanted to become a secondary English teacher. The first day, she entered the small classroom carrying a packet of three-by-five cards and an armload of old, red-covered *English Journals,* which she put down on the round table where the five or six other English majors and I were seated. The assignment for the semester was to read articles from the *Journals* and summarize them on the cards. We were to save our cards, and at the end of the semester, if we had summarized the assigned number of articles, we would get an A. Each class period thereafter was a repetition of the first: she'd drop off the *English Journals,* leave the room, and come back to collect them at the end of the hour. Over the years, when teachers tell me that they hated their education classes, this is the kind of class I hope they mean. Our professor brought to her class a combination of qualities that make for terrible teaching. She was lazy, arrogant, and a purveyor of maddening assignments that demonstrated a disdain, if not outright contempt, for her students.

The director of the teacher education program fit another of the stereotypes that sometimes gives these department programs a bad name. He was an intense and jittery man who was totally devoted to his work and who wanted desperately to teach us everything he knew, believed, and loved about education. He had read a lot of books on teaching, and by the time I took his course, he had become totally infused with their jargon. The jargon of education can be embarrassing, and he spoke it well. Phrases like "felt needs" kept popping up in all of his lectures. "Felt needs" were very important to him. Even though he was a warm and lovable old soul, we mocked him. Because we felt sorry for him, but we all liked him, we did our best to translate his clichés into terms useful for us and help him make his classes work. We did this to protect him, but then again, who is to say that the ability to turn clichés into more vital language is not an important life skill?

Professor Verna Newsome was another matter altogether. Verna was an English professor with a strong traditional bent, and all by herself she made that year and a half I spent at Wisconsin State earning my Wisconsin Teaching Credential worthwhile. She was one of the great teachers who charted the course of my life. She was tall and elegant and always dressed as if she were setting out for an afternoon tea. She owned a large Victorian house near the campus that, with its dark and lustrous paneled walls, was elegant also. She was later to become a close personal friend. As a teacher, Verna was a gracious person whose gentle ways inspired excellence. Under her tutelage, I studied the history of the English language and English grammar and took the two-course sequence she taught in descriptive and expository writing. She taught me to love the English language, and she taught me how to write as Madison had not. She demanded the most of her students, and I responded. No matter how long it would take to do a particular assignment, I was determined to hand in something excellent. She had within her the teaching magic that I came to look for in others when I was directing the writing project. She had a way of making her students approach even ordinary assignments or exercises ("Write five descriptive sentences." "Write a description of a particular place from a particular perspective." "Write a description from a moving object.") as if we really were writers practicing our craft. Everything I wrote I treated as if writing had become my art. But there was something gamelike about this, too. She inspired another approach that skilled teachers I know encourage. She taught me to treat each assignment as a contest with myself, a problem I was eager to solve in the same way I had once approached geometry problems, the tougher the better.

I spent hours, days, working on assignments. I wrote from memory and from observation. I created my own exercises: I wrote short pieces that were pulled from imagined longer pieces; I imitated writers; I copied passages from accomplished writers, as Benjamin Franklin describes doing in his autobiography. More and more I began to write for the pure joy of it. I wrote stories and sketches, and again I started a literary magazine, *The Cheshire,* appointed myself editor, and published my first story.

Verna wrote a book, *Sentence Craft,* that, along with her courses, inspired in me an interest in the way the English sentence works, which has continued throughout my career. Her work and the work of another great friend, Francis Christensen, helped form a major part of my focus as a teacher, both in my own writing courses and in my courses on the teaching of writing. Over the years I've conducted a number of workshops on syntax and style for the writing project. Style and syntax became my niche, just as other writing project teachers have formed their niches of expertise. I believe that the richness of our subject matter makes it possible— even necessary—for us to find areas of expertise. By sharing what we know best, we contribute to the general excellence of the profession.

The last time I visited Verna Newsome, then well into her retirement, she said to me, "The more I study the English language, the more I'm amazed by it."

⟿ *My Life as a Truant Officer* ⟿

I HAD ONE FURTHER EXPERIENCE during the time I was a student at Wisconsin State that had an important impact on my future career. In the fall of 1952, I accepted a part-time position as truant officer for the Milwaukee public schools. I worked out of an office in Lincoln High School, where I was student teaching one class. My job was to hunt down chronic absentees in the urban twelfth and fourteenth wards, the area served by Lincoln High. I spent much of the final semester walking the streets in Milwaukee's oldest and poorest residential area, looking inside what were at one time large and mostly elegant red brick family homes but which had been converted into apartment houses. Occasionally I'd walk into a house that had not been divided in this way, yet several families lived in it—one family per room— with sheets and blankets hung up over clotheslines to separate one family from another and provide some privacy.

When I visited these grand old homes, I saw sights I never could have imagined. On one occasion, I entered a large room filled with old mattresses that were placed so tightly together on the floor there was no walking room—just mattresses.

Another day I climbed a dark stairway, every step piled high with old newspapers. A foul stench filled the space, so strong I gasped and began breathing through my mouth. A smiling, silent woman opened the door to the apartment I was looking for. Behind her, the living room was filled with bottles, old unwashed bottles on every flat surface and tabletop in the room, bottles large and small, milk bottles, beer bottles, bottles of all kinds loaded in boxes on the floor. I didn't know how I was going to get to the boy I was looking for—I took for granted that he was in a bedroom. I told the woman I was looking for her son, and she led me around the bottles to the bedroom, where I was left alone with a thin, sickly boy lying in a bed. The mother smiled but never said a word. I left the apartment and went to my office in Lincoln High as swiftly as I could to report what I had seen.

I didn't know what to do many times during my semester as a truant officer. I was too immature, too inexperienced, too sheltered to handle that job at that time and in that world of Milwaukee's twelfth and fourteenth wards.

I saw poverty close up for the first time. I had never seen rats the size of suckling pigs or toilets without a seat in the middle of a kitchen floor. These experiences bothered me greatly and certainly stretched me. How could a boy whose only home was a second-story room filled with dirty and smelly mattresses be expected to go to school? What chance did a boy have living in a putrid apartment and in the care of a mother who seemed to me clearly mad? I found children too sick, too disoriented, too isolated and lonely to even find their way to school. Everything I experienced in my work as truant officer was new to me, and it left me with a wider perspective and a deeper sensitivity. Successful schools would not just be about smart, well-trained teachers and rich curriculum. For schools to work, the society would have to work.

⤳ First Teaching Job: A Shaky Debut ⤳

Like many teachers, I was a total failure in my first teaching job—teaching seventh-graders in Watertown, Wisconsin. I lost total control of four out of my five classes. My fifth class was an oasis. It was a class of mostly girls. As sometimes happens with beginning teachers, I found myself concentrating on this easy success and ignoring my failures in those classes where I didn't really know what to do. In my one successful class, we spent a lot of time reading poetry—children's poetry as well as other poems that were musical and rhythmic. We also wrote poems and put together our own anthology, which was introduced by a long chain of couplets about the class, the teacher, and the students: "Our teacher's name is Mr. Gray / who always has so much to say." We printed copies for each student, and I printed others to show my friends on the faculty. I was pleased and proud of this effort, a pride only somewhat diminished when one of the teachers told me that not all of the poems were original.

Meanwhile, such unrelenting chaos continued in the other four classes that at least once a day the principal dropped in and took a seat in the back of the room in the hope that his presence might help. Even the superintendent of schools, whose office was in the same building, visited my room regularly on the pretense of adjusting the shades. Nothing helped.

The trouble started when I told my classes to call me Jim. Soon, my students and students in all of the other classes in this school of seventh- to twelfth-graders were calling me "Jim." When I walked down the halls, a chant of "Hi, Jim, Hi, Jim" would start up. When I went to evening basketball games and the students saw me walk into the gymnasium, a chant of "Hi, Jim, Hi, Jim" would greet me from the grandstand. I heard the same chorus when I walked down Main Street on a Saturday morning.

Yet when I started teaching in Watertown, Wisconsin, even though I was failure in that first job, I knew I belonged, that I was in the right world. I loved the old, square, three-story red brick school, which looked like so many others I had seen throughout the Midwest. I liked the oiled and shiny wood floors. I loved the unmistakable school smell. I loved my classroom and loved having it all to myself. I soon grew to know many of the teachers, and a group of us went out to dinner every night, Monday through Thursday. And even when I knew I had to move to another school so that I'd have the chance to start all over again, my love for schools had become permanent and deeply felt. I was determined to become a good teacher.

ᔄ Coming of Age in the Classroom ᔄ

In the fall of 1953, following this first semester of teaching, I moved to California, where I thought I could get a job from my uncle Fritz, then superintendent of schools in San Mateo. He wouldn't give his nephew a job, but he did line up interviews for me in three East Bay districts: Richmond, where the principal, Mr. Gray, wanted me to take over the school newspaper; Berkeley, where they wouldn't continue the interview once I told them that I was considering other districts; and San Leandro, where the principal made no effort to disguise his high regard for my uncle. During that interview, I told the principal and vice principal all about my disastrous first semester. They seemed more amused than put off. Rather than reject me for my failure, they talked about how great the opportunity would be for me at San Leandro High School. I was delighted. My candidness on this occasion and others has served me well. Teachers establish their credibility by admitting their mistakes. Forthrightness is a characteristic I came to treasure in teachers we interviewed for the writing project's summer institutes.

Because the school district was new, having recently broken away from Oakland, most of the teachers were near my age, only a few years older than the students. Teaching classes with students who looked almost as old as I was made a big difference. Unlike my experience with seventh-graders, I had some inkling of how their minds worked. Even though I still had problems and would continue to have problems learning to teach, I was determined to make it. Except for the names given to the different courses, there was no set curriculum, and this control over my own courses would, in time, give me the freedom to succeed. Even though I was still very much the beginner, I was treated as a professional by the administration and by other teachers. I talked daily with my colleague Leo Ruth—who also taught at the school and with whom I was then sharing an apartment—about my teaching, my classes, and my problems. Leo, who is still a good friend, was patient and listened to my agonies night after night. He calmed me, and when he could, he gave me well-thought-out advice. I also met frequently with Ralph Sherlock, the English department chairman and a fellow University of Wisconsin graduate, and I gradually began to learn how to teach.

Sometime during my second or third year at San Leandro, I made radical changes in what I was teaching and the way I was teaching it. I became disgusted with literature texts with their three-poems-per-poet approach and with their questions at the end of each work, which seldom ventured beyond just the facts:

"How many witches were in Macbeth?" The grammar composition texts were worse. To me, they were wrong-headed and unfriendly books that taught students to recognize an indirect object but did not teach students to write. Some teachers can work up the enthusiasm necessary to motivate a class of teenagers with such books, but I am not one of them. So I left the textbooks on the shelves in the textbook room while I began to experiment with new ways to teach literature and composition. Initially, I focused on short fiction and close reading. We also read a play by Shakespeare each semester, and as I experimented, I found that the more Shakespearean plays we read, the more the students liked Shakespeare. I picked up on a principle that came to guide my teaching as well as the future work of the writing project. When teaching or learning new skills like reading Shakespeare or writing well, a teacher needs to keep at it. One way we learn to read and write is by reading and writing regularly and frequently.

I was creating my own curriculum. I had an investment in what I was doing because I was following my own beliefs, and the successes I had with the changes and refinements I made boosted my confidence. I took great pleasure designing my curriculum from whole cloth. I believe every teacher wants this, to have some say in what he or she teaches, to have his or her expertise recognized and honored.

One day in my fourth year, the principal came into my room and invited me to give a talk, at a breakfast meeting, to the whole faculty on "The Art of Teaching." Maybe he thought I needed some solid recognition, but whatever his reasons, he clearly thought I was a good teacher, and I was very pleased. But I also knew this was a stupid idea. After only a few years of teaching, I was hardly in a position to make pronouncements on such an ambitious topic, particularly when the audience would be my colleagues and drinking buddies. So I thanked him for the compliment and refused the invitation.

⇥ The Classroom as Library ⇤

WITH THE POPULATION EXPLOSION in California in the mid-1950s, districts couldn't build schools fast enough. San Leandro solved the problem by moving in Depression-era Civilian Conservation Corps portables, and I was lucky enough to get one, a huge room with old wooden walls and a smaller semiprivate area in the back that I could decorate any way I pleased. I began decorating the walls of my new classroom with bookcases made from discarded but clean wooden apple boxes. I would get up early on a Saturday morning to scout the market produce delivery areas before the boxes were picked up. I chose the best of them and nailed them to each other and to the walls. I painted them white and added red-and-white shelf paper, so we would have an easier time moving books on and off the shelves. This obsession continued over my remaining years at San Leandro High School, and in time I had the wall opposite the windows and the wall behind my desk lined with book-filled apple-box bookcases up to six feet tall.

All of this was done with a purpose. I expected students in all of my literature classes to plunge into this library. I became more and more convinced that the best thing I could do for the general mix of high school students was to cultivate their love for books. I believed then, as I still do, that if students become readers at an early age, they will be readers for life. They will never be bored, and if they go on to college, their extensive reading will serve them well. So I began a consuming hunt for the books I wanted to have on those shelves. Buying books is one of the things, like eating and sleeping, that I must do in life, so I moved many books from my apartment library to my school library, and on Saturday mornings after my hunt for more apple boxes, Leo, who taught nonreaders how to read, and I began hunting for more books at the used bookstores in Berkeley and at Salvation Army stores. Each time, without too much looking, I quickly filled a large paper bag with many of the titles I was looking for, frequently in hardbound, for a dollar per bag.

Then I discovered more ways to stock my classroom library. I began seeking donations from the students in my classes. No one complained. I would go up and down the rows each day during the first days of each new semester with a blue-and-white metal camping cup in hand asking for donations to help build our library. The students found it amusing, but it did get their attention. They began caring about the number of books we had in the room. Some students donated their own books and books from their homes. I remember one afternoon being invited by a boy who was not even a student in my class to rummage around in his family's book-filled garage. There were books on shelves and in boxes, and I came away with dozens of major works—all in hardbound—plus a complete set of the novels of Sir Walter Scott. As the students and I settled in to this new program, I started each day talking for about ten minutes about the book lists I had created and annotated. One was a sixty-plus-page, historically arranged, annotated list of English novels (shades of Miss Popham). I put together oodles of lists: American novels, Russian novels, English and French novels. As I talked about the books, I would keep my eye on the class to sense which books seemed to interest which students, and when I finished my book talk, I'd go to our classroom library, pull out the books, and give them to the interested students to check out. For the rest of the period they would read and browse in our growing library. On Fridays we all got into a large circle, and the students, one by one and informally, talked about the book they were reading. Everyone had a chance to give a book talk. These Friday sessions had a magical effect. I remember one boy laughing with such delight over Charles Finney's *The Circus of Dr. Lao* that others began reading it. This happened over and over again. One year, after a book talk about *Vanity Fair,* a group of girls decided that they would read only long books—*Gone with the Wind, Kristin Lavransdatter, Anna Karenina.* One group of boys decided to read only Russian novels, and another group decided to read only the unknown novels of major writers.

Later, after I had left San Leandro and began teaching at the University of California, Berkeley, I remained obsessed with this approach to teaching literature. On one occasion, Ed Farrell, my officemate at UC Berkeley for many years, and I were awarded a federal grant to create and film experimental classes for the Demonstration Secondary School that UC Berkeley's School of Education conducted each summer at Oakland Technical High School. Ed would teach poetry and drama and I would teach fiction in back-to-back, two-hour classes to the same group of soon-to-be tenth-graders, and I would use this opportunity to make a film of the wide-reading approach I had developed and refined at San Leandro High School. My plan was to teach this class exactly as I had taught it at San Leandro—with my book lists, my book talks, my approach of encouraging students to read widely and freely in books they wanted to read, and with time set aside each week for the students to talk to one another about what they were reading. The one great difference was that this class would be filmed.

To keep the filming from interfering with the day-to-day class work, we thought it wise to film indirectly, with cameras that could be operated by cameramen in an adjoining room. But setting up this operation and making it work took far longer than expected, and it was already dark on the Sunday night before classes would begin and we weren't ready. Everyone was exhausted. The books for the classroom library were still in boxes stacked in the middle of my classroom, and my plan of unpacking and arranging them in the bookcases beforehand was more than any of us could deal with, so we left everything the way it was and went home. I decided to have the students finish the work the next day.

Ed and I had recruited the students by visiting all of the junior high schools in the neighborhood and talking to principals and English department chairs about what we would be doing. That Monday morning, twenty-plus students of various backgrounds showed up at 8:00 A.M. for their first two-hour class in fiction. They knew as soon as they entered the classroom that something was wrong. Piled high in the middle of the room was a huge stack of cartons, which had been delivered by Berkley Books, Inc. As part of our grant, I had received a thousand dollars to buy the classroom library that I wanted, and with paperbacks selling at twenty-five and thirty-five cents per book in the fall of 1963, I had bought a lot of books and filled a lot of boxes.

I welcomed the students and gave them their directions:

- Empty the cartons in the middle of the room, and take the empty cartons out into the hall.
- Put the books into the bookcases according to the bookcase labels: American novels in these cases, English novels in these cases, Russian novels here, all other novels here, short stories here.
- Put a three-by-five card into each book with the title written at the top and numbers from one to five down the left-hand side. These would be our library cards, so I would know who was reading what at all times.

I discovered that I had introduced them to a game that none of them had played before. They dived in, ripping the covers off the cartons and dumping the books in a pile in the middle of the room. When they saw a book they had already read, they'd shout out, "I read this one!" "This one was really good!" "Hey, look at this cover!" It was a joyful and noisy operation. Students kept coming to my desk asking: "Is this a Russian novel or what?" "Is this American or English?" "What's this one?" And I helped them categorize everything from "Other European" to "Current Popular."

When they were well into it, a few students and then more students began to pick out books they thought they might want to read, and small piles of bright-covered paperbacks began to appear on some of the desks. By the time all of the books were arranged in the bookcases with three-by-five cards visible in each, every student was sitting at a desk reading one of the books he or she had chosen. The room was totally quiet, and that's the way it stayed for the next thirty minutes. I sat at my desk watching, without saying a word. I had told them nothing about the class. I had not suggested that they start reading a book if there was time left after all our work was done. As I watched these students reading, I was filled with wonder and a deep joy. Nothing like this had ever happened to me before. I was as silent as they were, but my mind was racing. Books had a power over those students that morning that I had never seen before, yet I knew without any doubt that if I had done the same thing in exactly the same way and under the same conditions with any other group of students, the results would have been exactly the same. It had all happened without any talk or any teaching from me. I knew then that this was the most successful single-class session I had ever had or ever would have. That magical morning was the absolute high point in my teaching career.

ᔐ *Adventures in Teacher Power* ᔐ

DEVELOPING THIS METHOD OF TEACHING LITERATURE was by no means the only thing I learned during my tenure at San Leandro High. In 1957, Leo Ruth became department chairman at San Leandro, and not long afterward a situation occurred that began to shape my view that the "top-down" philosophy that dominated university or school relations was no longer acceptable. Two district administrators informed Leo that they were going to bring in outside curriculum experts as consultants to plan a new secondary English curriculum. Leo refused. The administrators met with Leo again, and he said, "No. The teachers should do that work themselves!" They called meeting after meeting. They brought in a curriculum expert from Stanford and other experts in the Bay Area to talk to us, and through all of this, Leo said, "We want to do it ourselves." This standoff lasted until the district office, probably out of exhaustion, approved a plan Leo had submitted. It called for paying five of us the standard summer school salary to write a secondary English curriculum for San Leandro High School that we could all live with and benefit from. Leo has been a hero to me ever since!

San Leandro High School believed in "teacher power" without ever having heard or used the phrase. The teachers I came to know best were consumed by teaching, putting in long hours in planning and preparation to achieve the standards they set for themselves and for their students. It was taken for granted that teachers would do their best. Teachers talked to one another about what they were doing. I knew how Leo Ruth taught poor readers how to read, how Ralph Pomeroy taught poetry, how Lee Jensen taught biology, how Sam Levine taught drama, and how Ken Soares taught public speaking. The roots of the Bay Area Writing Project were firmly and deeply planted during my seven years of teaching at San Leandro High School.

ᔕ *Asilomar: Teachers Teaching Teachers* ᔕ

SHORTLY AFTER I ARRIVED AT SAN LEANDRO in the fall of 1953, I was invited to share an experience that greatly affected my understanding of the power of collective teacher knowledge. A number of my colleagues in the San Leandro English department invited me to join them at the Asilomar conference in Pacific Grove, around the bay from Carmel. I had never gone to a conference nor envisioned a place as unique as Asilomar: gorgeous rustic redwood buildings amid pine, redwood, and cypress trees at the edge of white sand beaches along the Pacific Ocean. Despite Asilomar's natural beauty, it was the Asilomar conference format that made and still makes this conference so special. Teachers sign up for a three-day study group that focuses on a single area of study. There's no other way to attend the Asilomar conference. I signed up for the group on composition. The leader, whose role was to keep discussion moving and lively, was Barney Tanner, an English teacher from Palo Alto. The rest of us were also classroom teachers, experienced and inexperienced. For three days I listened to excited and clearly committed English teachers share their ideas and practices, their successes and questions and concerns. Which works of literature generate fresh student thinking and writing? What do we do when a student misinterprets a text but writes well? On the drive back to San Leandro, I very happily talked through my notes from the weekend and announced, "I have eighteen new ideas about teaching writing, and all of the ideas came from other classroom teachers!"

⤶ *The Experts Speak; the Teachers Listen* ⤶

BUT NOT EVERY DAY WAS LIKE ASILOMAR. One afternoon toward the end of my career at San Leandro High School, our community of teachers was paid a visit so much in contrast to the sharing culture our faculty had developed that it came to symbolize all of the tensions that existed between schools and universities. A team of UC Berkeley English professors, Jim Lynch and Bertram Evans, were invited to address the English department. Lynch and Evans taught a course on the teaching of literature in secondary school, and Evans had published a book of dialogs, *The Dialogs of Elantius,* that presented their particular beliefs that students should be taught only great works of literature and that the reading of great works improves the lives of the readers, particularly if the readers are less able students. It's usually interesting to discuss a point of view about teaching with those who care deeply, as did both Lynch and Evans, and I certainly was an advocate for reading great literature. But there was no discussion possible that afternoon. The team was revved up, and they got right at it. In no time at all we were told what was wrong with the way we were teaching and how we ought to be doing it. I was outraged. What right did these two professors—or anyone, for that matter—have to tell me what I must do and think as a teacher! What arrogance! To tell me that I was doing a lousy job when they didn't know what I was doing! They did not know me, had never met me, and had never visited my classroom. They did not know what I believed in, what I taught, or how I taught it.

Later, when I joined the UC faculty, I came to know Lynch and Evans personally and, indeed, accompanied them on several school visits. I found they were caring men who were genuinely interested in helping kids to become more literate. Many teachers I know liked them and respected their work. But on the occasion of their visit to San Leandro, I did not see it that way. I was not looking at them as people; they became symbols to me. I saw two academics who had no interest whatsoever in tapping the knowledge of the top-flight English faculty sitting in that room. There wasn't even a hint that they believed there might be something to tap from this audience of teachers. There was no hint that they had ever once in their careers considered such an idea.

That afternoon I was not only unable to understand what I saw as the presumptuousness of two professors judging us without knowing us, but I was also outraged when it became clear that these two men believed there could be nothing about teaching worth knowing from just a roomful of teachers.

Since that occasion, I have met hundreds of academics who admire classroom teachers and treat them with respect. And, as the writing project presents itself as a university-school partnership, we, in turn, admire and respect academics and value their collaboration. Maybe Lynch and Evans on another day and in another situation would treat teachers as partners in a mutual endeavor, but on that day they didn't. The event remains a stain on my memory.

Early Consciousness-Raising

Over the years, the Bay Area Writing Project, as well as other sites, have collected a cadre of specialized workshop presenters. We have a maven for every writing education niche. You want someone who knows about portfolios, or writing-to-learn, or holistic scoring, or revision, or show-not-tell, or techniques for teaching writing to English-language learners, or on and on? We have that person. But in the early days, when we were preparing to start an inservice series and there was a hint that the group might be difficult, we would send a generalist, Keith Caldwell, who had a knack for softening up a tough group of cynics. Here Keith writes of a bit of consciousness-raising he did for us early on.

I was moved to ask the first fifty groups I worked with in California and around the country one question: Which university or other institution of higher learning taught you how to teach writing? In no case did any teacher—from Maine to Arizona or New York to Los Angeles—raise a hand. None, zero, zilch. Not one person could tell me where they had been taught to teach kids to write, to do the job they were hired to do and were doing. No department of education, anywhere, had taught them. We had an entire nation being taught by untrained teachers who had nowhere to go to get trained to teach writing. Where did the teachers learn? From their own teaching and from one another, from a rich oral tradition and by using their wit and genius as teachers to learn the art and discipline of teaching from experience.

I asked that question to over one hundred groups.

I also asked if any of them had ever been asked to share or demonstrate what they did and what they knew. None and none. I do not know how that situation had come about. We floated on rafts of textbooks, and we should not have had to. I must give the writing project the credit for turning the problem around; there was no other influence on the scene.

Chapter Three

UNIVERSITY DAYS AND SOME DETOURS

IN 1961, I WAS INVITED TO COME TO UC BERKELEY as an English supervisor. Two years earlier, Leo Ruth, who recommended me, had also been invited to Berkeley to work with teacher trainees. Berkeley's School of Education's Teacher Education Division had a long-standing policy of hiring successful, well-thought-of classroom teachers as supervisors to train graduate students in its credential programs. This was a teachers-teaching-teachers idea, rare for its time and transparently sensible. Effective and experienced classroom teachers, rather than professors, did the job of teaching and supervising beginning student teachers. I accepted, and every year for the next fourteen years I taught fifteen beginning English teachers how to teach and visited them in their student teaching classes. Year after year, I had groups of gifted young teachers who, I always thought, could have chosen any career, but chose teaching because teaching is what they had always wanted to do. After the second of these years, however, a challenge materialized that was to contribute substantially to my thinking about schools and teaching.

DoDDS: From Bureaucrat to Advocate

IN 1963, I WAS OFFERED THE CHANCE to serve as director of English, language arts, and reading for the Department of Defense Dependent Schools (DoDDS) in Europe and the Middle East, a position that, due to a periodic reorganization cycle that reorganized me out of a job, was to last but eight months. But it was during this productive time that I began rehearsing ideas that became key to the writing project model.

However, my arrival at the DoDDS European headquarters in Karlsruhe, Germany, was delayed four months, so when I arrived on the job in January 1964, I faced a backlog of mail and an empty out-basket. My immediate supervisor was new also. I was given little direction about the nature of my job, so I simply dove into the pile of work, thinking that this was probably what I should do as director of English for all the American schools scattered over much of Europe as well as Ethiopia. It took me very little time to recognize that what I was doing was mostly of little account.

As a result, and tempted by one or two invitations in my in-box, I stopped doing it and began visiting schools instead. I took a train to visit the Paris Elementary and Secondary School. Entering this school, I realized that I was observing these classes with a status I had not had before. I was an administrator, not a teacher or even a supervisor of student teachers. On that first visit, I observed a wonderful kindergarten teacher who started each day by playing a very engaging piece of classical music for her students. She featured the same piece each morning for one week and then selected another for the following week, continuing throughout the school year. The back wall of her room was a huge map of the world that charted, with colored string, the travels of each child in the class. This teacher—I've forgotten her name—had lived in Paris for years on the beautiful Île de la Cité in the Seine, and she delighted in taking her classes on field trips to the many spots in Paris she knew they would like, such as the famous pet cemetery. There was always an assignment on each field trip, something particular that the children had to seek out and look at, such as a particular stained-glass window in Notre Dame. She joyfully told me of parents filled with wonder to hear their five-year-olds talking about a Paris the parents themselves had neither seen nor heard about, and on other occasions singing out the great melody of the first movement of Tchaikovsky's Violin Concerto.

On that same first day, I also visited the class of a teacher whose style greatly disturbed me. She was teaching from a teacher-proof textbook programmed by the publishers so that everything the teacher would say and ask of her students was printed in bold black ink, and everything the children would say in response was printed in red ink. I could hardly contain myself as she later calmly described what she had been doing, with total acceptance and satisfaction.

After each of my visits to DoDDS schools, I reported what I observed, the great and the less great, to the principals who were meeting me for the first time and, as I learned later, were expecting little from me. My commentaries helped them by confirming their judgments of truly excellent teachers as well as supporting their assessment of the less able. But I was coming to realize that if someone could help the by-the-book teacher I had observed, it would not be me in my position as DoDDS director, or even the school principal, but rather the teacher whose kids were humming Tchaikovsky.

I began to visit DoDDS secondary schools in Germany and France. I soon discovered a pattern. There was in fact a DoDDS secondary English curriculum. It consisted of grammar lessons and composition text on Tuesday and Thursday and the literature text on Monday, Wednesday, and Friday. That was the paper curriculum.

But as I spent less time in the Karlsruhe office and visited more schools, I discovered more about how this government school district worked. I learned that despite the rigidity of the published curriculum, some principals in this huge school district were going their own way, with varying degrees of insight. By far the worst example was a "creative" principal at Fountainbleau Middle School. The man had read a book on schooling that ignited him, and he had implemented a flexible weekly schedule of classes as described in the book. He was excited by what he had accomplished and excited that I was there to see it. But I soon learned he had consulted no teachers in devising his little education utopia. What I saw was an unintentional parody of a plan based on flexible scheduling. One teacher told me that the small class I observed met only one day per week, and small class size be damned, she hardly knew who her students were. I also observed large class instruction—at least as long as I could stand it—where I heard a teacher lecture on verbs, hardly the stuff to present to seventh- and eighth-graders in a large lecture hall. After class I asked her what else she would cover in these twice-weekly large classes. She told me adjectives and adverbs were next.

After each visit I wrote a narrative report describing what I had witnessed and sent it to the assistant superintendent in charge of curriculum. On this occasion I reported in detail on the complicated time and motion schedule the principal had devised but did not understand—a schedule he had created without once consulting the expertise of the teachers who would need to dance to his beat. Making visits, talking with teachers whenever I could, I wrote reports that told the teachers' stories to the assistant superintendent.

I became more and more comfortable with the job, more confident, and more than ever dedicated to exposing enforced top-down situations like the one at Fountainbleau. In the summer of 1964, I invited some of the impressive teachers I had met to Karlsruhe to put their expertise to work on a five-week grades 7–12 curriculum workshop. There were seven teachers, including Joan Gibbons, a former Los Altos, California, English teacher who would become the director of English after me; she still holds that position, and now supervises all DoDDS areas worldwide.

During those five weeks, the eight of us wrote the new English curriculum for the DoDDS Secondary Schools. We developed a resource guide for teachers that included study guides for literature for each grade level; techniques for teaching language, composition, and the genres of literature; and annotated book lists. English teachers were given a potpourri of options, which we presented in a three-ring binder so that teachers could add new material. With this guide, DoDDS classroom teachers were, in effect, given control of their own classrooms, free to design their own plan of study for their students.

The work of these teachers that summer foreshadowed the structure of the writing project summer institutes that were to come. Each teacher was in charge of writing particular items, with the others free to add material of their own to any of the content areas. All of the teachers served as an ongoing response group. We were teaching one another and being taught by our colleagues. We were stimulated and enthusiastic all summer long.

ᗒ *Helen Strickland: Educational Visionary* ᗒ

IN AUGUST 1964, I RETURNED TO CALIFORNIA and resumed my work as student teacher supervisor at Berkeley. One morning, the dean of the School of Education introduced me to Helen Strickland, director of curriculum and staff development for the Placer County Office of Education. Helen was one of the toughest and most innovative and influential educators I have ever known. She was as multifaceted as a diamond. When she retired, after a career of good work, she did everything she had always wanted to do: she rode a donkey around the volcanoes in Iceland, she climbed to Base Camp Three on Mount Everest, she took the trans-Siberian railroad across Russia, and when she was finally ready to settle down, she moved to Tahiti.

Helen began her career as an elementary teacher in Kentucky, earned a doctorate along the way, and finished her career as the director of curriculum and staff development for Placer County in the foothills of California. When I met her, she was looking for three consultants (in literature, composition, and language) to help her put together her plan for an English project that would serve English and language arts teachers in northeast California's Area III, which encompassed thirteen counties. Helen and I hit it off immediately, and she invited me to join her team as literature consultant. This project, which had begun in 1963 and went on for a number of years, was a seminal experience for me. Like the teachers would at the Bay Area Writing Project Summer Institutes later, these were teachers working together; they came from colleges, universities, and K–12 classrooms, and all were recommended by their county administrators. The focus of this project was clearly on the teachers, with Helen constantly honoring and encouraging them.

This fairly large group of teachers met together in the late afternoons and evenings on a regular schedule during the school year. In some ways, our Area III work resembled the better inservice programs of the times. We began each session with a lecture from a distinguished speaker Helen had lined up. I remember Wallace Stegner's lecture on literature, in which he spelled out the unique features of the short story, as one of the best I had ever heard. Then these large group sessions were followed by small group sessions that relied in part on the expertise of teachers. As the leader of the literature group, I sometimes introduced particular approaches to the teaching of literature, but mostly I broke up that group into smaller groups, where individuals shared ideas and practices with one another.

We began our work in the fall, and by springtime an increasing number of participants were beginning to give workshops to other teachers in their local counties. I have a wonderful memory of an all-day series of sessions conducted at

Mount Shasta in a school built halfway up the mountain. Our car caravan full of Area III teachers was greeted by the Mount Shasta teachers and others from the surrounding area, many looking like they had just come out of the woods or down from the mountains for the first time in months, with their ragged beards, heavy boots, and flannel shirts. The project teachers were celebrities that day, for it was the first time the local teachers had ever attended inservice programs that were conducted by real classroom teachers.

I was shocked one day during the summer of 1968 when, at a meeting in her home, Helen announced she was retiring. I had an immediate sense of loss, for she had come to mean a lot to me and had taught me so much. When I think of her now, I see her with her boots on, ready to walk the trails in the foothills, a country woman who never forgot her rural roots. Brusque as she could be at times, she was a remarkable organizer and teacher. She was a powerhouse who respected classroom teachers as she respected some academics, and called on both teachers and academics to help her improve the preparation and teaching of classroom teachers throughout that vast area in which she worked. She was an uncompromising leader whose impact on me has been deeper and more lasting than anything I could have known at the time.

⤳ The English Teacher Specialist ⤳ Program: Canceled in Advance

IN MANY WAYS, the California English Teacher Specialist Program, which ran from 1968 to 1970, was an extension of the Area III English Project; it developed the Area III project's teacher-to-teacher model and extended the program to all of the counties in California. In the early summer of 1967, George Nemetz, a former participant in the Area III project and now consultant in English for the California State Department of Education, hired me to come to Sacramento to help him plan the new teacher specialist program. The plan was to select outstanding teachers of English from grades one through twelve for training as English teacher specialists, an expert cadre of classroom teachers who would conduct inservice workshops throughout California. At the end of the process, 110 specialists were selected.

During their training, the specialists heard from and consulted with many distinguished authorities in literacy education, including major figures from both the United States and the United Kingdom, among them James Moffett, Wallace Douglass, Andrew Wilkinson, Geoffrey Summerfield, Bob Hogan, and William Glasser. At the end of the training program, we had a cadre of California's most distinguished English teachers prepared to work with state teachers.

But in 1970, two years after the program began, a new California superintendent of public instruction was elected, and the English Teacher Specialist Program was canceled. I knew then, and have certainly been aware since, that such cancellations are common. When new superintendents or deans or principals come on board, they have their own ideas of what needs to be done; as understandable as this may be, I've frequently thought that these administrators must have all attended the same course on "How to get rid of absolutely every good program that existed before you became boss."

But perhaps the new state superintendent was right about one aspect of the English specialist program. Operating as a state entity, we were trying to cover too much ground. This is why we decided, when we began planning the Bay Area Writing Project, to limit our geographic focus to the nine counties surrounding the greater San Francisco Bay Area. With 176 separate school districts in the area, there would be work enough to do without thinking of how we might serve the state or the nation. Through my experience with the English Teacher Specialist Program, I had discovered how difficult it was to initiate and manage a major program for a state as large as California out of a single office in Sacramento.

⌒ The NDEA Institutes: New Idea, Old Model ⌒

BEGINNING IN THE LATE 1950S, education reform was on the national agenda, but it was reform less motivated by concern for our students than by the need for survival as a nation. In 1957, Sputnik, the world's first artificial satellite, began its journey circling Earth, and this alarming USSR breakthrough opened the vaults of the Treasury to support educational reform. Though one congressman wanted to pass a resolution condemning the Soviet Union for this un-American act, others concluded, more realistically, that something had to be done to ensure that America's next wave of scientists didn't fall behind. A range of federally funded education reform programs quickly surfaced—such as New Math, PSSA Physics, Chem Study, New Biology, and more.

After many new programs to improve the teaching of math and science were in place, Jim Squire, at that time executive secretary of the National Council of Teachers of English (NCTE), directed an intense campaign to find similar federal funding to improve the teaching of English. He sent a copy of the NCTE monograph *The National Interest in the Teaching of English* to the Commissioner of Education and commenced a vigorous personal effort that secured federal funding for English and English teachers on a par with what had previously been made available only to teachers of mathematics and science.

The resulting National Defense Education Act (NDEA) English Institutes, located at key locations all over the country and in operation during the late 1960s and early 1970s, were immensely successful for their time. The institutes were popular, but highly competitive, and the teachers selected for these residential summer programs, through the screening of exacting applications, were honored and feted and paid handsome stipends on top of their free room and board. The faculties at the various centers, selected by the institute directors, typically included at least one or two of our most highly regarded scholars in the field of English studies. At the Hawaii Institute, for example, Richard Larson invited Ian Watt, professor of English at UC Berkeley and author of the highly acclaimed *The Rise of the Novel,* to teach the literature course. Guest speakers on the circuit included such names as Noam Chomsky, Wallace Stegner, and Louise Rosenblatt.

However, the institutes inevitably followed the traditional summer school model, and the carefully selected classroom teachers were treated as students. It never occurred to anyone—including the teachers themselves—to tap the knowledge that these experienced teachers had brought with them or to explore what it was that made these teachers the excellent teachers they were. It was simply the way things were done at universities: professors taught the courses, and students took the courses, wrote the essays, and took the exams. The professors did not think of doing things differently, and the teachers, having taken scores of university classes, didn't either. And—because the institutes were run as summer sessions—when the last day was over, the institute was over. There was no thought of keeping these teachers together in a network of some sort; there was no thought of having these teachers teach other teachers. Such notions, now key elements of the writing project, never surfaced.

∽ NDEA Hawaii Institute: I Become the Professor ∽

IN 1965, RICHARD LARSON, the director of the University of Hawaii NDEA Institute, invited me to join his summer staff as the director of the institute's colloquium, to test the materials generated by Project English—an earlier NDEA project that brought together key scholars to develop materials in English studies that could be used by classroom teachers. The course was also intended to explore new approaches to the teaching of English. Although my experience by now had taught me the best way to proceed—when working with skilled teachers, honor teachers—I paid no attention to my experience. Instead, as I planned the colloquium, I put everything that I had come to believe about working with teachers out of my mind. I prepared to teach what was to have been the best course I had ever taught on the teaching of English, and I put myself at the center, even though I knew the teachers I would be working with were carefully selected and successful public and private school teachers from the Hawaiian Islands. Beyond the fact that these teachers had gone through a rigorous application process, I knew nothing about them, and I made no effort to find out, no effort to tap what they knew about the teaching of English or to have them demonstrate their approaches or best practices. I knew better, but somehow I got caught up in the aura of being a part of this federally funded institute, teaching at the University of Hawaii, team-teaching with Ian Watt, the English professor I admired above all others.

About halfway through my course, I sensed that all was not right. I became increasingly troubled. There were tensions in the classroom. And then something clicked, and I knew what I should have known all along. I tried to make amends. I asked two or three teachers if they would like to demonstrate something they had had success with in the classroom. But it was too late; I had waited too long and had given off too many wrong signals. There was no great interest on the teachers' part in doing anything at all.

This whole experience still embarrasses me. I vowed that if I ever had the opportunity to work with teachers again, I would do everything I could to make up for that Hawaiian disaster. I would never again work with a group of respected teachers as if I were the lone expert.

⌐ NDEA at UC Davis: ⌐ Standing the Institute on Its Head

AS HAS HAPPENED SO MANY TIMES DURING MY CAREER, luck played a key role in what happened next. I was invited to teach the colloquium course again, this time at the NDEA Institute at UC Davis, and I had the opportunity to replay my experience of the previous summer, this time getting it right. Again the conditions were ideal—a distinguished faculty, an exceptional group of teachers (mostly from California), impressive guest speakers, great stipends, excellent accommodations, great camaraderie, and a program of faculty-teacher parties, dances, lunches, and receptions that would last throughout the summer.

On meeting the teachers on the first day of the institute, I told them that I was going to try an experiment. We were all going to teach this course together. I told the teachers about the Hawaiian experience, the mistake I had made by not treating experienced teachers as colleagues, and I promised them that things were going to be different this summer at UC Davis. I asked them to prepare demonstrations of their best practices or approaches, the things that worked best for them as English teachers, the strategies that had led to their being recommended for this institute. I told them I would do the same, and together we would learn from each other.

As in Hawaii, they had access to all of the materials from Project English and were free to make use of them if they wished in their demonstrations or in the joint class portfolio that I had assigned, a resource guide of their own teaching practices for all of the participants to have and use.

The differences were striking. Never before had these teachers had such an experience, neither in school nor in a university. Never had they been asked to talk about what they knew to other teachers. Never had they been recognized and celebrated as knowledgeable experts in their field—the practice of teaching English.

I had success at Davis because I turned my course on the teaching of English over to the teachers. By turning the NDEA model upside down, by recognizing the expertise of the teachers the institute had brought together, I made it work for all of us. *I had the model that was to become the model of the writing project*. Over time, I've added to it and refined it, but I've never changed it. I knew what had to be done. And knowing this gave me confidence and strength as well as understanding—and a focus that has never blurred.

There were great classroom teachers in the schools who knew how to teach writing; they knew what they were doing and why they were doing it. They could be identified, and in the summer institute, they would teach one another their own best practices. In the process, they would learn how to teach other teachers and then go out and do it. It would be a teacher-centered model.

⤺ *Beyond Miss Popham* ⤻

AFTER THE UC DAVIS NDEA INSTITUTE, I knew I was going to start a new and better staff development program, but I wasn't sure whether it would focus on literature or writing. Both, as commonly practiced, were in sorry shape. Literature teaching was anthology based for the most part, and I had dumped that approach as hopeless early on in my career. The teaching of writing was simply ignored.

In the mid-1950s, when I began teaching writing at San Leandro High School, teachers who taught writing corrected the papers they assigned by identifying the errors students made with coded marks in the margins and by writing comments at the bottom of the last page. There was no talk of drafts, neither first drafts nor final edits, no discussion of writing as a process, and rare use of writing groups. There was no thought given to revision in such an approach—reading first and second versions of the same paper would simply double the time it took! Instead, students were asked to look over their corrected papers and note the mistakes they made so that they could do better next time.

In my literature classes, I had filled the room with books, but I had assigned no writing. I believed, perhaps mistakenly in retrospect, that if I was prodding my students to love literature, I was doing my job as an English teacher. After all, Miss Popham had assigned no essays. I also taught a senior college-prep English class. In this class, it was expected that students would be doing some writing. So every Friday, my students wrote an essay in class. It was common practice in my class and in other classes like it in Bay Area high schools to use old UC Berkeley Subject A tests for these in-class writing assignments. I had dozens of these tests, each giving the writer ten or more topics to choose from on such subjects as "Should Red

China be admitted to the UN?" and "How would you build the perfect hen house?"

Even though I was dealing with only one batch of essays a week, it took me a long time to correct them, and I was always behind. As the stacks of papers on my desk at home became increasingly numerous, the task of grading became so onerous that I eventually didn't even try. I read them, wrote "See me" at the end of each paper, and then considered them marked, corrected, and graded. I didn't notice any great harm as a result. The students never complained. And it was far easier for me just to read through their papers and call the students up to my desk to talk about what they had written than to try to write out everything I wanted to say. I've thought of this class quite often since, and while I realize I didn't know much about teaching writing at that time, I now think that what I had the students do was okay, and perhaps even better than okay. By writing an essay a week, they wrote about twelve different essays each semester, and they were expected to talk with me about their papers rather than merely translate my scrawled symbols. They were well prepared to pass the Subject A test, and they had experience in the kind of writing that would be expected of them as college freshmen.

I also taught one class of creative writing. For this class, a colleague recommended a book that he had found useful, *The Fabric of Fiction* by Douglas Bement and Ross M. Taylor. The book is filled with wonderful stories that suggest starting points for beginning writers, with numerous models for each. One approach became a mainstay with me: "The Deep Well," an idea that came from a comment Henry James once made when asked how he came by his ideas. He said he stored them away in his mind and brought them up again by tapping his deep well of recollections. I've used this "Deep Well" assignment ever since in one variation or another when I ask students to write their own stories or re-create their own experiences.

I began to use models regularly, whatever my assignments, reading them aloud and commenting on whatever I wanted my students to note. I read some of the descriptive pieces I had written in Verna Newsome's class, and as students' own pieces came in, I used them too as models, reading them aloud to the class and commenting on the various features I liked. In doing all of this, I discovered a key to teaching writing that has *always* worked for me; that is, the more I read aloud and sincerely praise the pieces I like, the more such pieces I receive. On occasion

I asked these creative writing students to write anything they wanted in any genre that interested them. I read these pieces, many of which were poems, to the class without comment and without naming the author, and had the students respond as I had with other pieces. The students kept journals that they gave to me to read about every two weeks. I didn't write in these journals, but I spent a good deal of time talking to the writers about what I read. Of course, none of these techniques was original with me. Good teachers, for instance, have always read aloud and praised student efforts. But I was identifying practices that worked for me, that I would be willing to share with others. The sharing of best practices became a cornerstone of the writing project.

⇆ *Sentence Modeling:* ⇆
Learning from Rachel Carson

WHEN I WAS INVITED TO TEACH writing classes at UC Berkeley in addition to my work as a supervisor of English education, I relied on some of the same techniques I had developed in the San Leandro creative writing class: helping students draw topics from their "deep well," relying on the "See me" that led to a productive revision, and reading aloud and praising student work I admired.

Then I encountered Francis Christensen, a professor of romantic literature at the University of Southern California, in the fall of 1963, and I soon added another strategy to my repertoire. I was present when Christensen read "The Rhetoric of the Sentence," a just-completed piece about writing, to a packed audience of teachers at Asilomar. Though Christensen was a specialist in Wordsworth and the romantic poets, through a circuitous route he had been drawn into the study of how English sentences are made in the works of modern British and American writers. I knew I was hearing something new about syntax (and style) that would change the way I would teach writing thereafter.

Christensen described how he became interested in this study when he noted that certain syntactic patterns commonly used by the current writers he was reading—Rachel Carson, Philip Roth, the staff writers of *The New Yorker*—were either dismissed or ignored by the authors, past and present, of grammar and composition textbooks. Immediately, on returning home, I began looking at sentences in the works Christensen had mentioned and, as my fascination grew, into the works of other modern writers. I began making lists of sentences that interested me and categorizing them under the headings: verb phrase, adjective phrase, noun phrase, adverbial phrase, and absolute phrase. And as I continued to read and follow my own research, I designed a simple approach to introduce these patterns to my students. From the first day I introduced this method, it had an immediate impact on the quality of my students' writing. The sentences of my students began to look a lot like the sentences of those professional writers they were modeling.

Because I have been so involved with sentence modeling, I have been sensitive to criticism of this strategy over the years. Why, some ask, do we want students to ape professional writers when they should be developing their own voices and styles? I think these critics are missing the point. The object of sentence modeling is not to create students who believe they are accomplished writers because they can mimic the sentences of Truman Capote; it is to help these young writers better understand what Capote and other modern writers are doing.

One also hears that if students read widely, they will by osmosis come to understand the range of stylistic possibilities. I don't argue this point. Ever since Miss Popham changed my life with her reading lists, I have understood the benefits of the reading life to writing. But there were not and are not many classes in secondary schools or even colleges that encourage diving into books in the way I encouraged my students to.

In recent years, younger children have been put in school situations where wide reading is part of the curriculum. But in general, students who develop a writing style because they are readers come from the most privileged homes where books are part of the culture. Sentence modeling opens up the secrets of style for students unlikely to get it elsewhere.

The other criticism of sentence and paragraph modeling is that these are mere exercises, that quality writing needs to start with an idea, not a structure. There is truth to this, and if my efforts had begun and ended with form, I would not have served my students well. My goal was to have students take in the possibilities and use them to say confidently what they wanted to say. Toward this end, I would send them out into the world to observe. The sentences, below, drawn from longer pieces, make general use of the forms used in sentence modeling exercises, but do not mimic specific sentences. Here one student reports on a visit to a funeral home with two aged neighbors.

> *They are old now, dressed in black for these occasions, filing past the wooden box, peering meekly at their own inevitable fate, then turning their eyes away—sad eyes, tearful eyes, a dark sea of sorrow.*

Another catches the attitude of a friend she is profiling when the two meet a strange man in a Berkeley coffeehouse.

> *I don't think she could understand him any better than I could, but she laughed anyway, crinkling up her eyes and flipping her long, shiny hair over her bare shoulders.*

∽ Student Writers Out in the World ∽

IN MOTIVATING STUDENTS TO WRITE, I relied heavily on "The Deep Well," on pulling up memories, but I also began considering ways students could use writing to observe the world here and now. My guide in this departure was *The New Yorker,* which I began reading in the 1950s. I was taken with writers such as A. J. Liebling and particularly Lillian Ross, who had tapped into a kind of reportage that was vital.

Ross and her colleagues generated a crisp, lively style that I believed my students, particularly with their grounding in Christensen-like sentences, could emulate. At about the same time, Tom Wolfe described something new and gripping in the world of modern nonfiction he called the "New Journalism." He told his audience of teachers he thought this new nonfiction was "the most important literature being written today," and he published an anthology of this nonfiction called *The New Journalism,* which included such writers as Rex Reed, Gay Talese, Truman Capote, Terry Southern, Hunter Thompson, Norman Mailer, George Plimpton, and Joan Didion. Wolfe described the new journalism as focusing on facts but making use of fictional techniques—scenes, characters, characterizations, and dialogue, as well as changes in point of view that allowed writers to be both active participants and outside observers, moving in and out of these roles. I came to see that my students could experiment with these and other devices in their nonfiction writing, looking in-depth at a subject just as the new journalist writers did.

Now I knew why I had saved those *New Yorkers* all those years. I used these back issues to prime the students' writing pumps. As with my reading class, I provided the resources but I allowed students maximum freedom in exploring what to do with them. Students wrote what they wanted, put together their own response groups if they were inclined, and handed in final drafts when they were satisfied with them. Most wrote two or three pieces, but a dozen or more students wrote five to ten. They had discovered, if they didn't already know it, that they were writers. Many read their pieces aloud, and I frequently set aside one or two pieces that I would read to the class because I couldn't bear not reading them myself. Students in these advanced composition classes embarked on many adventures in search of topics in which they could immerse themselves. Here I am only able to quote a small piece of one. This is Ann Kipley's "Bob's Drive In," a detached Lillian Ross-like report of one night shift at Bob's in the Haight-Ashbury section of San Francisco in 1970.

> *In the summer of 1967 the phenomenon of hippie culture spread in every form, distortion and perversion imaginable into all parts of the United States, as fast as the media could carry it—and that's very fast. In April a Connecticut housewife asked "What's a hippie?" By June her sixteen year old son was one, complete with a new album by Country Joe and the Fish and a brightly flowered shirt he wouldn't have been caught dead in a few weeks before. As pierced ears and long hair and love beads appeared in every middle-class neighborhood in the country, parents began worrying about things they had never worried about before, "Please, and I want you to tell me the truth," a Cleveland mother pleads, "Have you ever smoked LSD?"*

> *The fatherland of hippiedom, as all the mass media proclaimed psychedelically, was the Haight-Ashbury district of San Francisco. "If*

you're goin' to San Francisco, be sure to wear some flowers in your hair; In the streets of San Francisco, you're gonna meet some gentle people there . . . ." This was the number one song on the charts; the good vibrations poured from AM radios coast to coast. Stories of life in the streets of the Haight reached mythical proportion. A huge migration of new-born hippies descended from all corners of the country, seeking the free life, the beautiful life under the sun with love and flowers for all. But it didn't happen. Amid the brutal realities of day-to-day survival in the city, magic is short lived.

Today the ghosts of this dream haunt the streets of the Haight. The faded, peeling paint of the storefronts, like ancient ruins of a long-dead civilization, barely reveal the once bright aliveness of the people who lived there. The streets are still filled with young people, but there is a deathlike air about them, wandering zombie-like along the sidewalks, trying to make a little bread by selling the BARB to passers-by, lurking in the doorways, pale and tired, rarely smiling, their eyes grown old. At the end of this sad street is Bob's Drive-in, open twenty-four hours a day, gathering place for those who find themselves cold and tired, in need of coffee and a juke box, in the darkest hours of the night.

A young man of about twenty-five is on his fourth refill of strong, bitter coffee. "There's a bunch of speed-freaks crashing at my place," he explains to the waitress. "Five of 'em. Can't stand 'em. So I got to stay up all night. They just rap, rap, rap. All night long." He shakes his head and lights another cigarette. "You know, a few years ago I used to take acid like everybody else, for the whole head trip, all that. Now, like tonight, I just take it to stay awake. It's no thrill. Just keeps me awake, you know? No cosmic energy, just energy to keep my eyes open."

He is one of the regulars. Most of the people in Bob's are regulars— either street people or bar people. The street people sit at the counter for hours at a time, smoking cigarettes, drinking coffee, playing the juke box. Some talk all night, others are quiet. Some leave then reappear several *times during the night, crying, "Hey, where's my coffee cup gone to? I was gonna have another refill!" One man, crew-cut, bearded, a black spot on his ear lobe where an earring once dangled, studies engineering from the pages of a correspondence course booklet. "Does anybody know how to change inches to feet?"*

With my students creating pieces like this, I knew I was on to something. They were observing and deftly reporting on subjects that mattered to them; they were writing varied and balanced sentences in a style more advanced than the writing of most undergraduates. They were, in fact, beginning to sound rather like writers for *The New Yorker.*

Chapter Five

THE BAY AREA WRITING PROJECT BEGINS

⤺ *The Writing Problem at UC Berkeley* ⤺

BY THE EARLY 1970S, my developing concept for a writing project was becoming increasingly timely. The faculty and administration at UC Berkeley were aware that more and more freshmen were entering the university unprepared to handle the writing that would be asked of them. Since the 1890s, UC Berkeley had demanded that entering students be tested on their ability to write, and until 1926, if they couldn't demonstrate such ability, the doors of the University of California were closed to them. In 1926, the Berkeley campus began admitting students who failed the writing test, but it insisted that such students enroll in Subject A, a remedial course in writing parallel to the remedial courses in Latin (Subject B) and Mathematics (Subject C) also required at that time.

The Subject A test, given to all incoming freshman, asked students to write an essay based on a prose passage that was written at a level they were expected to be able to read and understand. The students had three hours to complete their essays and were allowed the use of a dictionary. Judged on the basis of their writing, a substantial percentage of the students taking the test in 1973 seemed to be poor bets for survival—*Time* reported this figure as 50 percent—without the help of Subject A's intensive catch-up course in college writing. Students required to take Subject A paid a fee and received no credit. Each week they wrote a college essay, which was read closely by a Subject A lecturer. Students would be passed out of this class when they began to write at an acceptable level.

The university was particularly upset because under the guidelines of California's Master Plan of Education, UC Berkeley and all of the other campuses of the University of California system were drawing their freshman classes from only the top 12.5 percent of high school graduates. Berkeley's freshmen were bright students, but in the early 1970s, most had limited experience writing papers about ideas.

One source of this problem was clear. The schools were not talking to the university, and the university was not talking to the schools. As someone who had taught in the schools and was now at the university, I thought I was in a position to introduce these two alien universes. So I launched a plan to encourage university teachers and classroom teachers to begin to work together. I brought together a number of teachers I knew—classroom teachers from the schools and professors and instructors from UC Berkeley—to discuss what might be done to improve the state of writing in the schools. I knew the teachers through my long and close association with the Central California Council of Teachers of English; the professors I knew through my ties to the English, rhetoric, and Subject A departments.

Our first meeting in the fall of 1972 was held in that magnificent redwood hunting lodge that Bernard Maybeck, one of this country's great architects, designed in 1902 for the Faculty Club. The room was arranged in a square of large tables so that everyone could see one another. The teachers and professors, most of whom didn't know one another, began to describe the problem as they saw it. Blame for the sorry state of affairs was lobbed, like a hand grenade, back and forth across the table, and at times it was vicious. The university teachers said, "If you had taught them how to write, we wouldn't have this problem." And the school teachers said, "They're your students, so why don't you teach them how you want them to write and stop blaming us?" The high school teachers were a tough bunch, and they weren't pleased at being lectured to. The college teachers were angry and mocking. I had not anticipated this. But I didn't want to give up on this idea of bringing teachers at different levels together to talk about a common problem. I called another meeting. The second meeting was no better, so I called it quits. It was clear that out of this particular mix of strong personalities no productive, collegial university-school partnership would emerge.

ᐸ Taking the Plunge: The Launching of BAWP ᐳ

AT ABOUT THIS SAME TIME, I was undergoing a personal epiphany. I had been supervising student teachers for thirteen years, and I was, in a word, bored. My students were great—smart young people who could have succeeded at any profession. I loved the conversations we had after I observed their classes. The problem was that they were beginners. Like the piano teacher who has watched her novice students make the same mistakes one too many times, I felt I needed a change. I was coming to reflect on my total experience in education: the community of teachers that had evolved at San Leandro, the dialogues of the teachers at Asilomar, the teacher-driven curriculum reform at DoDDS, the power of teachers teaching teachers that I witnessed at Davis, at Area III, and at the NDEA Institute at Davis.

I thought about all the successful teachers I knew who were doing inspiring work behind the closed doors of their classrooms, and I contemplated the potency of a structure that would allow these teachers to share the theory and strategy of their best practices and then make this knowledge available to others, including the beginning teachers I was working with.

I was contemplating this idea one day as I drove the twenty miles it took to visit a student teacher I had placed in Ignacio Valley High School. When I arrived at the high school, I couldn't find a place to park, so I turned around and drove home. I spent the rest of the afternoon making notes, outlining the staff development project that would become the Bay Area Writing Project. The next day, I went to see Assistant Dean John Matlin and told him what I wanted to do. Almost immediately, he arranged with the dean of the School of Education to give me released time to get this work started. The university, of course, was troubled by the latest "crisis in writing" as reflected in the Subject A scores, and here was an idea that might reverse this decline. No one had put forth a competitive idea. We were filling a need, so it happened that, from the beginning, the Bay Area Writing Project was recognized and supported by UC Berkeley's top levels of administration: the provosts and deans of Letters and Science and the professional schools, and the dean and assistant dean of the School of Education.

At the disastrous Faculty Club meetings, two eager allies, Bill Brandt, professor of rhetoric at Berkeley, and Albert "Cap" Lavin, English teacher from Sir Francis Drake High School in Marin County, had surfaced. Both had a keen interest in writing, both had published texts on the teaching of writing, and Cap had the distinction of being the only American classroom teacher invited to the famed

Anglo-American Dartmouth Conference that had brought American and British educators together to examine the current state of English studies. I wanted the proposed writing project to be codirected by an academic in the field of writing and by a classroom teacher of writing. The three of us began meeting regularly, with others joining us on occasion. Cap and I met frequently, in the late afternoons, and always in one or another of the Bay Area's beautiful spots—our favorite was Sam's Cafe in Tiburon, with its mammoth deck overlooking San Francisco Bay. What would this Bay Area Writing Project be and do? We reviewed what we knew about what had worked. The idea of a summer institute surfaced as I recounted my Davis summer. Other concepts emerged from casual brainstorming. "We ought to have them write," one of us said. And that offhand remark led to what people now refer to as "the community of writers that is integral to the summer institute."

It was also important to us that teachers learn about changes in the field of teaching writing. In the early 1970s, there was an emerging body of knowledge from research and from the classroom practice of successful teachers. While we were beginning to know more than we had ever known before about writing and the teaching of writing, many classroom teachers, working as they do behind the closed doors of their classrooms, knew little about these developments and had no easy way of becoming informed. We knew that a familiarity with the work of Francis Christensen, James Moffett, and Ken Macrorie, for example, would help them think about their practices.

From the beginning, I thought of the writing project primarily as a staff development program to improve the teaching of writing, but my idea of staff development had little to do with what went by that name in the schools at the time.

When I was teaching high school in San Leandro, "staff development" was accomplished in one day, the first day back after summer vacation. Staff Development Day started with doughnuts and coffee and a lot of happy chatter, then a coming together to listen to an "inspirational" speaker, who was followed by a long lunch break at a favorite local restaurant for a good time, good food, and good talk with friends that one hadn't seen since early summer. This day was always great fun, but as staff development, it was a zero.

I was aware that teachers, particularly secondary teachers, were increasingly cynical of most school staff development efforts—principals hiring some expert who would talk about particular problems facing the school, such as classroom management. These "workshops" were random and isolated and—a major sore point—always mandated. Teachers would reluctantly attend the meetings, usually sitting in the back of the room, sometimes hoping for the best but almost always expecting the worst. The value of many of these meetings was equivalent to the cowboy singers and sleight-of-hand magicians some districts once hired for school assemblies. There simply were no regular and well-planned staff development programs that were focused on teaching and the content of teaching.

The situation in higher education was no better. Universities and colleges offered programs that led to the credentialing of beginning teachers, and some offered advanced credentials, but—outside of summer school courses that were open to the general public—universities did not offer systematic and ongoing programs for the continuing education of classroom teachers. Because of the difficulties of satisfying university requirements governing graduate student enrollment, there seemed no possibility of doing more for teachers.

Cap and I could easily assume that teachers at all levels, with very few exceptions, were not trained to teach writing when they began teaching. Elementary teachers had been taught to teach reading, and secondary English teachers had been taught the history of English literature. But neither elementary teachers on their way to their credentials nor secondary teachers, as far as I knew, had ever been required to take a course in the teaching of writing. In 1973, I called Bob Hogan, a friend and former colleague, who, at that time, was executive director of the National Council of Teachers of English, and asked him if he knew of any college or university that offered a course in the teaching of writing. He was intrigued but told me he couldn't think of any offhand. He told me he'd look. When we spoke again, he told me he hadn't been able to identify a single university or college that offered such a course! He assumed that if writing instruction was touched on at all it was as part of a general methods course.

We knew that the teachers who were teaching writing were doing so out of their own personal interest in writing and their belief in its importance. We also knew that they had trained themselves to teach writing through their day-to-day, trial-and-error experiences. These teachers—successful teachers of writing who knew and believed in what they were doing—were the teachers we wanted to identify and use to teach other teachers. We saw what reporters were labeling "the crisis in English writing" as basically a crisis in staff development. Student writing was not going to improve until the teaching of writing improved.

I knew that the knowledge successful teachers had gained through their experience and practice in the classroom was not tapped, sought after, shared, or for the most part, even known about. I knew also that if there was ever going to be reform in American education, it was going to take place in the nation's classrooms. And because teachers—and no one else—were in those classrooms, I knew that for reform to succeed, teachers had to be at the center. It became a burning issue with me that teachers were not seen as the key players in reform or as the true experts on what went on in their classrooms.

We wanted a project that focused on teacher-to-teacher exchanges, teachers coming together frequently to talk about what they were doing. We had no thought of packaging the ideas that rose to the top as the "Bay Area Writing Project" approach to the teaching of writing. We were not looking for any sure-fire formulas to peddle. In the early seventies, when writing instruction was starting to emerge from decades of neglect, any attempt to design a model curriculum would have been foolhardy and premature. We were contemptuous of publishers' efforts to design teacher-proof materials. Many excellent materials on writing already published by Project English, an earlier reform effort in the mid-1960s, had had little impact nationally on improving student writing abilities or the teaching of writing.

That writing, as fundamental as it is to student learning, had been so long neglected in this country has always been a puzzle to me. Scholars, of course, depend on the written word. The examination of texts is the stuff of English departments, yet professors within these departments whose major interest was composition and writing were in a distinct minority and frequently treated as second class. We see this neglect when we consider the traditional use of the word "literacy"—which has meant the ability to read, not the ability to read and write. There are some signs of change, but the exclusion of writing from consideration as a literacy skill is a habit that for some has been hard to break. I recently received a flyer from *Highlights for Children,* a magazine for parents that focuses on the learning skills children will need if they are to succeed in school. The flyer asks, "Are You Giving Your Child the Building Blocks?" and offers an illustration of each block. There are blocks for Listening, Reading, Creating, Thinking, Reasoning, Observing, and Comparing—but no block for Writing. In the illustration, happy little children are playing with all of the blocks. I felt sorry that the Writing block, wherever it was, was not allowed to be a part of the game.

⌒ *Our Friend Rod Park* ⌒

ROD PARK, PROVOST AND DEAN OF THE COLLEGE OF LETTERS AND SCIENCE, was concerned about the continuing writing problem that had surfaced again at Berkeley in the fall semester of 1973. While he knew that social problems—unlike scientific problems—were generally ones you work on rather than solve, he wanted to get started working on this particular problem. It was one of the many coincidences in the history of the writing project that that very fall our plan and model were in place, and we were eager to begin working with Bay Area teachers. One of the many faculty members who had participated in the early planning meetings, Bill Brandt, was also that fall an assistant dean of the College of Letters and Science. Bill mentioned the project to Park, who, within the week, invited me to his office. This meeting turned out to be the beginning of a close and enduring tie between Rod Park and the writing project and the beginning of major financial support for the project from the top levels of UC Berkeley administration. Within a short time, George Maslach, provost of professional schools, and Chancellor Bowker were also involved. The impact of Park's early support cannot be overstated. Without that support, it is likely there would never have been a Bay Area Writing Project.

Rod Park is a complex and highly principled man who, throughout his career, has been willing to reject unacceptable compromises. He is as close to a Renaissance man as anyone I have known—he is a competitive Transpac sailor (both crewed and single-handed), owner of a vineyard, a former overseer of Harvard, and a researcher in plant biology who, while serving as provost and dean and the vice chancellor, continued his research on photosynthesis and on squash proteins, which could be modified by genetic engineering to kill insects and thereby increase crop yields. But what Rod Park is best known for is his restructuring of UC Berkeley's thirteen biological sciences and related science departments into three new departments: Integrative Biology, Plant Biology, and Molecular and Cell Biology. With Chancellor J. Michael Heyman, he ran the successful campaign that raised over $100 million to house the new departments in two new science buildings and the completely rebuilt Life Science building. From its inception in 1974 to completion in 1994, the restructuring of these departments took twenty years of political and financial effort.

Park has recently retired as chancellor of the University of Colorado, Boulder and is using his free time to build his own airplane and to establish a new vineyard (the Rockpile Vineyard) in the coast range of northern Sonoma, seven miles beyond commercial power lines.

Either because of or in spite of his New England private school and Harvard background, Park is a populist at heart. As I eagerly described the project during that first meeting, he immediately, instinctively, understood the intent behind the Bay Area Writing Project model. He knew that the university could not simply tell the schools what to do, and he knew that the only way UC Berkeley would solve its writing problem was to collaborate with schools in a working partnership focused on improving student writing for the mutual advantage of both the universities and the schools.

Park believed the proposed Bay Area Writing Project, involving as it did teachers from the schools as well as from the university, could in time be the answer to the soaring enrollment in Subject A. Within days, he talked Chancellor Bowker into providing thirteen thousand dollars, even though, as he indicated later, he had to do a little arm twisting, since the Chancellor thought "teachers won't go for it." With this money, the Bay Area Writing Project began operations, and its first summer institute was conducted the following year, in 1974. Park offered me an open door to his office during this time, and the two of us met regularly thereafter for short, productive sessions.

Rod Park hosted a breakfast for the first group of summer institute participants, and after welcoming the teachers to the university, he described UC Berkeley's current Subject A situation. His audience was uneasy. This was not a topic the teachers wanted to talk about. One fellow, Keith Caldwell, blurted out: "You've got a problem? Well, solve it yourself. We've got our own problems to worry about." Park delighted in this give and take, but it was clear in the first meeting that many of the teachers, even though they had accepted the project's invitation to attend, were still extremely wary of this new university program. These were leading teachers who were successful in their own classrooms—quick to react to any hint of criticism, any hint of condescension, or any attempt from anyone outside the classroom to tell them how to improve their teaching. A few had participated in earlier university efforts to "improve the schools" and had become cynical of such efforts.

Rod was always ready to offer practical help to the project. During the first institute, fellow Miles Myers taught an experimental class on campus to Oakland school students that was videotaped and hooked up so that we—in the room next door—could watch whenever we pleased. When the Oakland bus drivers went on strike, making it impossible for the students to attend class, Rod Park chartered a bus and had the students delivered to the campus at the university's expense! At the end of the first institute, with all but five hundred dollars spent, Rod offered to pick up any additional expenses for the invitational dinner Cap and I wished to hold for a group of key Bay Area administrators in order to describe the services the writing project could now offer their schools and teachers.

Over the first three years, Park approved approximately $198,000 of university funding to develop the project, and in the late 1970s, working closely with Vice President Donald Swain, he set in motion the process that eventually led to the writing project receiving its direct support from the California state legislature. In later years, Rod Park frequently referred to the writing project as his "baby."

The First BAWP Summer Institute

THERE WE WERE—TWENTY-NINE OF US, counting the codirectors and myself—on a Monday morning in the summer of 1974, the first day of the first invitational institute of the Bay Area Writing Project.

Present in the room were Miles Myers, the Oakland high school teacher who would one day become executive director of the National Council of Teachers of

English, and Mary Ann Smith, the young woman who twenty-five years later would serve as codirector of the National Writing Project, as well as her team-teaching colleague, Jo Fyfe, a future associate director of the project.

There also were Bill Brandt of the UC Berkeley rhetoric department, who believed the key to strong writing was a carefully crafted topic sentence, and Sandy Seale, who was teaching her inner-city students to "code switch" long before the term was coined. Also present were future BAWP codirector Mary K. Healy, then a middle school teacher and Ph.D. candidate who had studied in England with the great literacy theoretician and researcher James Britton, and Cap Lavin, the legendary University of San Francisco basketball great who was in the process of becoming a legendary teacher of English.

Walking into the room, one teacher, Joan Christopher, could not believe her eyes. "I really didn't think anyone would be there," she told me later. "I was thinking maybe I was the only teacher in the world who cared about teaching writing."

This was an exciting but very bumpy time as we began to bring together the key elements of the model.

We were reluctant to ask everyone to give a demonstration, but the teachers who did show us their successful classroom practices confirmed our belief that the summer institute would cross-pollinate the successful teaching of writing as perhaps no other structure could.

Barney Tanner, the high school teacher who had led our group at Asilomar years before, gave a presentation on coherence. It was the kind of smart, ordered, and useful presentation one might have expected from a man dedicated to prodding his students toward successful academic writing.

But the presentation by Mary Ann Smith and Jo Fyfe, who were team teaching at Loma Vista Intermediate Junior High School, must have given Barney something to think about. In their classroom, they had been using the James Moffett *Interaction* series, which drew on booklets and activity cards, readings and prompts, and which introduced students to many forms of creative and real-world writing: letter writing, autobiographical writing, playwriting, and limericks, for instance. Mary Ann and Jo were committed to Moffett's key pedagogical idea: students need to experiment with genres, finding topics that interest them and working at their own pace. They explained Moffett's ideas and showed us examples of student work and a video of their own classroom in action. This concept was far ahead of the thinking of many of the high school and college teachers present at the institute. They, like almost all teachers at the time, had for the most part operated behind closed doors. We had brought together the most talented teachers we could find, yet as I was to understand over time, even teachers of this caliber have a lot to learn from one another.

One demonstration in particular opened our eyes. Kate Blickhahn, a teacher at Sir Francis Drake High School in Marin County, who would become principal of a neighboring school, demonstrated the concept of holistic scoring. This process allowed student writing to be assessed and ranked according to an agreed-upon rubric and in comparison to other students. It had been used at College Board readings for some time. However, it was a concept foreign to most classroom teachers. Not everyone present that day felt comfortable with the idea that a piece of student writing could be assessed without marking it up. But Kate explained that the purpose of holistic scoring at the school level was not to comment on an individual student's mastery of subject-verb agreement, but to give teachers, departments, and schools information that they could use to strengthen their writing programs. Everyone present that day took away from Kate's demonstration something they had not thought of before.

Though the key elements of the summer institute were in place from the beginning, we made some major mistakes. For instance, during the first year of the summer institute, we failed to include elementary teachers. We were so focused on the secondary-only NDEA model and on our goal to establish a project that would improve the writing levels of high school graduates that we didn't even consider the idea of a kindergarten through university mix. We should have known better. The need to attend to writing crosses all grade levels. Therefore, the work of all writing teachers on the kindergarten through university continuum is equally important to all other writing teachers. By the second institute, we had corrected our error and included teachers at all grade levels. We understood that teachers are naturally curious about the learning in other classrooms and at other grade levels, and yet they seldom have the chance to find out what's really going on in any classroom other than their own.

I remember one twelfth-grade teacher who introduced his demonstration by stating that it probably wouldn't be of any interest or use to anyone but the other senior high school or college teachers, a remark he came to regret. "Don't tell me what won't work in my classes!" the elementary teachers told him in so many words. After another demonstration, a teacher responded with what she thought was the pointed criticism: "I could do that with my fourth-graders!" But most present understood that yes, she could, but eleventh-graders would come at the same learning from different intellectual places and different levels of experience. This is one reason eleventh-grade teachers and fourth-grade teachers are able to share ideas. Whenever an elementary teacher asked me what time the doors to Tolman Hall, where we met, opened in the morning, I knew exactly what was going to happen. When we walked into our room on such a morning, we would see a room transformed into a replica of the teacher's own classroom, sometimes complete with puppets to play with, hats to wear, horns to toot, and whistles to blow. College teachers were fascinated by elementary teachers, and a bit envious also. They couldn't get over the color and decoration of their classrooms—all of it of educational interest—and the joy of these rooms compared to the totally sterile rooms they taught in, which usually had no decoration at all and nothing on the bulletin board but one old flyer for a concert held years earlier.

The Bay Area Writing Project model created an environment where both academics and classroom teachers could appreciate each other. Professors of English and of English education worked as partners and colleagues of classroom teachers. For teachers, BAWP was a university-based program that recognized—even celebrated—teacher expertise. For academics and teachers alike, the Bay Area Writing Project model managed to reverse the top-down, voice-from–Olympus model of so many past university efforts at school reform.

During the first summer, four faculty members from the department of rhetoric were summer fellows, including Bill Brandt, who became one of the project's initial codirectors. The guest speakers were all UC Berkeley faculty members, one of whom was Josephine Miles, who cared so much about what we were doing that she attended the project every morning. Miles was a distinguished professor who had been awarded the statewide title of university professor. She was a major American poet who was interested in all aspects of language and learning. Throughout the five weeks, she fully participated by giving a presentation and writing a position paper, which BAWP later published together with all of her other essays on writing and thinking.

I prepared a detailed schedule that covered everything we would be doing, including the day and time each teacher would give his or her demonstration, and naturally we were off-schedule even before the first week was over. Much of what we did during the first years was experimental and tentative. Now we require all participants to do a teaching demonstration and to write and share their writing. Some teachers never did make a presentation, and some were very slow in letting others see what they had written. Feeling our way, we didn't believe we were in a position to hold to rigid requirements.

Similarly, we became ambivalent about another of our initial requirements, that all summer fellows conduct a voluntary workshop for the teachers in their own schools or district during the follow-up year. We were concerned about the Prophet in His Own Land problem, but also, as the first invitational summer institute ran its course, we became aware for the first time that all of the great teachers we had brought together were not going to be equally great teachers of other teachers. We were finding out that teaching teachers was an altogether different art form, and an exceptional seventh-grade teacher is not necessarily going to be an exceptional teacher of seventh-grade teachers. Some summer fellows did not like to give presentations and never would; they would do something else to stay involved. Many simply needed more time and practice before they were ready to face other teachers.

LEARNING FROM EACH OTHER: K THROUGH COLLEGE

The summer institute is a space where those who might have once considered themselves strange bedfellows become colleagues with a shared mission. Here Teacher-Consultant Ellen Hitchcock comments on this phenomena.

My thoughts, which once would have been unembodied and lost, I now hold open for inspection. My journeying companions now are persons I would not have wanted to travel with—teachers of high school and college, professors of philosophy and religious studies, published authors. I once would have silently stepped aside and allowed them to pass me. But now through our common concern for our common students and our frequent dialogues, I am a member of a community, and I find that we talk more of our uncertainties along the way than proclaim any joy of having arrived. This has given me confidence to write. Life is no longer so secure, but I have become able to move farther, to begin to see the old in light of the new and the new in light of the old.

$\sim$

Early Interest in the Bay Area Writing Project

THINKING BACK ON THOSE EARLY DAYS, I understand that much of the early success of the writing project can be traced to being in the right spot at the right time. The right spot was a major and highly esteemed public university such as the University of California, Berkeley with its long tradition of public service. The right time was the mid-1970s, when the "Why Johnny Can't Write" stories began to appear in the nation's press: *Newsweek* published shocking samples of students' (and teachers') writing; *Time* reported that the decline in writing abilities was not just a problem of entering freshmen at UC Berkeley but a problem at universities nationwide; *The Chronicle of Higher Education,* in the report "The Crisis in English Writing," published similar findings; and in 1975, the press began reporting stories documenting a decline in SAT scores. As reporters investigated these stories, they also began asking what was being done in the nation to attack these problems, and as they looked around, they found the Bay Area Writing Project was the only visible program in place.

As national concern grew, so did interest in the writing project. The resulting press coverage brought—in addition to letters, phone calls, and invitations to speak—a steady number of visitors from other universities. The visitors—professors and teachers—returned to their own universities and states interested in starting something similar. Three representatives from Duke University and Durham County, North Carolina, visited the 1975 summer institute and returned to North Carolina determined to set up a similar project at Duke University—the first new site based on BAWP. Next, the Oregon Department of Education invited Cap, Miles, and me to Portland, Oregon, to describe Berkeley's writing project to educators who might be interested in what BAWP was doing to improve student writing. The large number of people who attended this meeting turned out to be a cross section of the state's educational establishment: classroom teachers and school and district administrators; faculty and administrators from the universities, private colleges, and community colleges; and other officials, such as the state superintendent of public instruction and the Department of Education coordinator of English and language arts. This visit led to the establishment of a third writing project site at Ashland, Oregon. Stories also began appearing in popular journals and magazines, such as *Readers' Digest, Education Today,* and *Woman's Day.* The *New York Times* sent a reporter to the Bay Area to do a story about the writing project. So numerous were the BAWP stories in newspapers and magazines that J. N. Hook, former executive secretary of the National Council of Teachers of English, once asked me, "Who's handling your public relations?"

THE SCHOOL-UNIVERSITY CONNECTION

By the late 1970s, the idea of the writing project seemed to be catching on. Faculty members at colleges and universities throughout the country understood that if significant educational change was to take place, schools and universities would need to form partnerships based on respect for each other's knowledge. Here Marjorie Kaiser, former director of the Louisville Writing Project and professor of education at the University of Louisville, writes about her first contact with the writing project.

I arrived at the University of Louisville in the fall of 1977 as the only English education faculty member in the School of Education. I was encouraged to develop courses and programs for middle and high school English language arts teachers, who prior to this time had only general education offerings and literature courses with which to build their graduate programs. I immediately established a tie with the language arts supervisors of the large Louisville public school district. I knew that unless teacher education at the university was intimately connected to the authentic schools and classrooms, my work would be irrelevant at best.

While my colleague Julia Dietrich and I dreamed about how we could truly make a difference for teachers in and around Louisville, Kentucky, during that fall of 1981, things had long been bubbling away in California, North Carolina, and Virginia. We did not know much about the Bay Area Writing Project at that time. Berkeley was not spending its limited funds on publications. In fact, most of the material we eventually received from Jim Gray was mimeographed. What I did know was what I had been doing: team teaching graduate courses with faculty in rhetoric who did not share my view of the value of teacher knowledge and the validity of wisdom that comes from classroom experience and from reflection on that experience. Rather, my team-teaching partner felt a responsibility to inform teachers of rhetorical theories that often had little connection to classroom practice.

In these classes, it generally fell to me to translate concepts and help teachers see how their teaching exemplified the rhetorical concepts presented to them. My role also included healing the wounds and preserving the self-images of teachers who were deflated and humiliated. Jim Gray spoke often, and still does, of this "top-down" approach. Too many with the responsibility of working with teachers, Jim said, view teachers as the "unwashed." The writing project was to change that. By honoring teacher knowledge, we view teachers as the professionals our communities expect them to be.

～

⤬ *The Project's First Grant Proposal* ⤬

IN THE SPRING PRIOR TO THE FIRST BAWP SUMMER INSTITUTE, I wrote a proposal that I submitted to eight foundations identified by UC Berkeley's Sponsored Projects Office. I was seeking funding for a project that had not yet begun, had not been tested, and had not been fine-tuned in any way. This derring-do was not lost on the reviewers. But I was optimistic. The writing project idea, however described, was exciting stuff, and in the proposal I referred to the "successful Bay Area Writing Project" from these earliest of our beginnings. But instead of receiving award letters that summer, I opened a series of rejection letters. The letter from the National Endowment for the Humanities rejected the proposal because it stated, "Writing is not a part of the humanities"! That caused some stir among the institute teachers.

But we did get a call from Alden Dunham, program officer at the Carnegie Corporation of New York, requesting a time when he could meet with us during a trip to California. We were all very excited; funding from just one of the eight was all we needed, and that the Carnegie Corporation of New York wanted to discuss our proposal was promising indeed. Bill Brandt, Cap Lavin, Merle Borowman (dean of the School of Education), and I met Dunham in the dean's office. Alden Dunham, elegant, impressive, and always to the point, was aware of the writing problem, as it was beginning to surface in various parts of the country, and possibly because he was a UC Berkeley graduate, he was clearly interested in UC Berkeley doing something to solve the problem. But he was not interested in our proposal. We had expected great news, but what we got from Alden was a critique on the proposal's shortcomings. Alden told us that he reviewed proposals by looking closely at the budget and the evaluation sections. Turning to the pages on evaluation, Alden asked, "Who wrote this? Who wrote this section?" I said I had. And Alden said, "Well, you know nothing about evaluation. Get somebody who does to help you write this section. Get Michael Scriven. He's at Berkeley. You can't get anyone better than Michael."

The meeting had not gone as we had hoped. I was embarrassed and disappointed. However, it didn't take long to realize that the sum of Alden's pointed comments really added up to an invitation to resubmit, but with the caution—and the directions!—to do it right the next time. Alden was right in rejecting the first proposal: the project was not ready to be funded, and we had accomplished nothing at all at the time we had submitted it. All of us were determined to submit a second proposal, but not until we had the working evidence to support our claim that we had an idea that would dramatically alter staff development education of teachers. It was not until 1976–77 that we wrote a proposal we were proud to submit.

~

On the last afternoon of the last day of the first summer institute, Cap Lavin and I really didn't know what lay ahead. Our effort to raise money had been a bust—seven rejections with one no-response out of eight submissions. It seemed unlikely that the Bay Area Writing Project idea of teachers teaching teachers would ever be realized. We had five hundred dollars remaining in our account. As we walked down to the parking lot, I turned to Cap and said, "Let's play 'Let's Pretend.' What would we be doing now if we had been funded?" We came up with the idea of blowing the whole five hundred dollars on a cocktail party and dinner in the UC Berkeley Men's Faculty Club for administrators from the schools and districts of the summer fellows. We could talk about the increasing seriousness of the writing problem. We could describe what UC Berkeley could do to help through the Bay Area Writing Project. The teachers could give us the names of key administrators who would likely be interested in what we would have to say. We talked it over with Rod Park and invited him to say a few words about the university's interest in working with schools as partners in this collaborative effort. Park liked the idea and offered to cover any expenses over five hundred dollars. We arranged for a private room in the Faculty Club, and all but one of those invited showed up. A waiter moved around the group with a tray of cocktails, and we began to have an enjoyable time. But I was new at this, and I didn't know about how the club handled such affairs. I hadn't given them a specific time to stop the flow of drinks and start the dinner service, so the tray of cocktails continued to make the rounds. One thing led to another as the mood became more festive than informative. Park said a few words, and I started talking about our plans, but I had the distinct impression no one was listening. However, I was to learn that a powerful idea can survive even missteps such as this. During that first year, BAWP received eight invitations to conduct workshops in the schools, though none, I'm afraid, from those in attendance at our dinner.

⟿ The Poly High Debacle ⟿

OUR FIRST INVITATION WAS FOR A WORKSHOP at San Francisco's Polytechnic High School. The principal invited me to bring some teachers who had participated in the first summer's program to talk to the Poly English department. I handpicked a strong group: Cap Lavin, BAWP's codirector; Miles Myers, a highly regarded Oakland high school teacher; and Flossie Lewis, a teacher at San Francisco's esteemed Lowell High School. Poly was not esteemed at the time. The papers regularly carried stories of faculty unrest and political and social tension on the campus. We weren't really surprised to find graffiti-filled halls. One inscription shouted at us, "Black is Beautiful; Yellow is Mellow; White is Shit." The teachers were waiting for us. I introduced my colleagues and began describing what the Bay Area Writing Project was all about. Suddenly, I was hit in the face by a paper wad thrown by some guy sitting in the second row. I ignored it and plowed ahead. Another paper wad. I was dumbfounded. Here we were, excited by this first invitation and the start, we hoped, of a long line of such invitations, and things were out of control. I reasoned that the situation could only get better, so I continued on. Another paper wad! Miles jumped out of his seat, went to the board, and began charting out some plan or model when someone else in the room shouted out: "Miles, go on back to Oakland where you belong!" Cap and Flossie were agitated. Cap, who suffered from angina, popped a nitroglycerin pill; Flossie was close to tears. Nothing made sense. The paper wad thrower shouted: "Gimme some pencils! If you want to help us, give us some pencils; we can always use pencils." The workshop was clearly over, and the four of us left the room.

We went across the street to a bar and tried to figure out what had happened. It should not have happened—not with the group I put together. All three of the teachers were well known and even revered in San Francisco. Cap was raised in San Francisco, where he had become a basketball legend. Miles was the senior vice president of the California Federation of Teachers (CFT) and the founder and editor of *California Teacher,* the CFT newspaper these teachers would have read in this strong union town. And Flossie Lewis was one of their own—one of the best-known, most-respected, and feistiest English teachers in town. It was beyond understanding why we'd been treated that way. The following week, one of the teachers called me. It seemed that the principal, a very unpopular *acting* principal who was at war with the faculty, had told teachers to show up for this workshop or else! The teachers showed up, not only to keep their files clean of reprimands, but also to get even by keeping this program from succeeding. They had nothing against us. They didn't know me. They did know Cap and Miles and Flossie, and they liked all of them. But they hated that acting principal.

That afternoon, we learned something about how to conduct a Bay Area Writing Project workshop and how not to. We vowed never again to have anything to do with mandated programs. Our workshops for teachers would from then on always be voluntary. If teachers didn't want to attend a Bay Area Writing Project workshop, they didn't have to, and we would make this very clear to teachers and administrators.

BAWP Bombs at Acalanes

THERE ARE MANY WAYS for a workshop to go wrong, and our next workshop for the Acalanes School District led to another misadventure. We had learned from the institute that a demonstration should not be entirely a lecture—that teachers in the workshop need to participate in the activity and respond just as students do. But the director of English of the Acalanes School District had another idea. I was so impatient to get something going, I was quite willing to do what the district wanted, that is: "Bring along your *hotshots,* four or five of your best teachers, not just one," the director said, "and have each of them briefly present what it is they do to teach writing." My instincts told me that a series of "Here's what I do" sessions would not work, but I knew how strong the teachers were, and I believed they might pull it off.

When I arrived at the district office, "hotshots" in tow, and entered our meeting room, I looked out onto a large room, cold and intimidating, filled with hard chairs set out in rigid rows. We faced a roomful of teachers who also seemed cold and intimidating. The director of English handled the introductions: "Teacher One, Teacher Two, Teacher Three, Teacher Four," he said, like his guests were contestants on the *Dating Game*. It was terrible. Our teachers had never faced anything like this before. They stood like sticks and hardly knew what to say, racing through their little talks like shy twelve-year-olds rather than the professionals they were. The next day, the director of English who had planned this fiasco distributed his curriculum newsletter to teachers and administrators throughout the district with the headline "BAWP BOMBS." I had the feeling he enjoyed putting that newsletter together, that he didn't mind at all seeing the "hotshots" lose a round. But we had learned another lesson. We had been asked to do something we did not want to do. We would not do it again.

⏤ *BAWP Discovers Its Inservice Model* ⏤

OUR NEXT WORKSHOP was to give us a model for the way we would conduct staff development from then on. Shortly after our early mishaps, I received a phone call from Vi Tallman, language arts coordinator for the Stanislaus County Office of Education, inviting me to conduct a UC Extension course on the teaching of writing. I had taught such a course on two previous occasions, and the county office wanted to continue this focus on writing. I told Vi a little about the new project we had at Berkeley and asked if she would mind if I handled the course a little differently this time by bringing along some of the outstanding teachers I had worked with during our recent institute. Vi didn't care how I handled it: "Anything you want. Anything." I made the trip to Modesto alone for the first session, but for each of the next nine weeks I arranged to chauffeur a different teacher from the institute—Miles Myers, Mary K. Healy, Barney Tanner, Cap Lavin, Keith Caldwell, and others—to the Stanislaus County Office on Thursday afternoons to conduct a three-hour workshop on the teaching of writing. I taxied each of the nine teachers to Modesto and back, a distance of about two hundred miles, took them all out to dinner, and from the thousand dollars I received from the county office for teaching the course, I wrote a personal check for fifty dollars to each of the teacher-consultants. I kept what was left as my share for serving as series coordinator. I thought this was fair all around. The early bookkeeping for the project was casual.

The audience of Modesto teachers had never experienced a program anything like this before: real classroom teachers demonstrating their own practices—approaches that fellow teachers had found successful in their own classrooms, one great teacher after another for ten straight weeks. Each week they were introduced to something new about teaching writing. Each week, in these three-hour sessions, they were given the time to experiment with these different teaching practices by doing the writing that students would do and then reading what they had written to other teachers in small response groups. After two or three weeks, I always gave some time over to the teachers so they could comment on how well these different practices had worked in their own classrooms in the preceding week, and these comments usually triggered further discussions about the teaching of writing.

For many, this was the first time they had ever come together with a group of fellow teachers to talk about writing and the teaching of writing. They loved it. They began talking about this new class to other teachers. A few local school administrators who were also beginning to hear about what was happening on Thursday afternoons began showing up. Vi became a regular guest along with one of her colleagues from the county office; even the county superintendent of schools attended one session. And so it began. BAWP was at work in the schools, and it had discovered its program design in Modesto: ten three-hour sessions, adding up to the thirty-hour UC Extension requirement for credit; a different classroom teacher as instructor at each workshop; and a coordinator who had an active role at each session. Over the next eight years, BAWP was invited to conduct four additional series in Modesto. The Merced County Office, having heard about this new UC Berkeley project at county office meetings, invited BAWP to do the same for the next two years—even Fresno County wanted BAWP, but the location was too far away.

Something was happening in the world of staff development. BAWP had established an aura. The telephone began to ring, and BAWP has been scheduling multiple inservice programs throughout the Bay Area ever since.

The Second Summer Institute

WE DID SOME FINE-TUNING for the second institute, to improve how we handled the demonstrations, the writing, and the response groups. But we didn't fine-tune enough. The second summer institute came close to being a total disaster, and that we didn't die right then and there clearly speaks to the power of the writing project's teacher-centered model to withstand and overcome even major disruptions.

The major disruption the second summer was a giant of a man with heavy curly black hair and a full black mustache who dressed—every day—in full black leather. He was also a magnificent writer whose prized possession was his motorcycle. That summer he wrote stunning pieces about the feel and thrill of riding fast on quiet country roads, windblown and free. He was an assistant professor of English at UC Berkeley with particular interest in seventeenth-century English poetry—and he was the most difficult human being I've ever had to deal with. Each morning he'd come late to the institute, stand in the doorway, glowering and scowling, looking for a chair, frequently disrupting whatever was going on—often nothing he was much interested in anyway. When he was bored or turned off, he sometimes would reach down into his black leather briefcase, pull out *Rolling Stone*, and begin reading. When he heard teachers say things about writing or teaching that he disagreed with, he would let us all know about it in some way or other, even to the point of yelling out "Bullshit!" He was, for many, totally intimidating. Yet, I couldn't believe that I couldn't fix things somehow. After all, I had twenty years of teaching experience behind me by this time, and I had dealt with difficult students, but nothing I had experienced in those earlier days helped me this time. He was clearly making many teachers uncomfortable, and on occasion had some close to tears. And yet while some found him a challenge, others found him fascinating.

One day early in the institute this problem professor gave a formal presentation, standing behind a podium that he had brought with him and reading a paper prepared for the occasion on the overuse of the verb "to be," the only time any teacher or any guest has read a formal paper in the history of the Bay Area Writing Project. His take on "to be" led to a heated argument. One teacher spent that evening looking up every memorable passage he could find in poetry and prose featuring some form of "to be" and made copies that he passed around to all the next morning. Some savored these electric exchanges, some were clearly attracted to him personally, and a good number of teachers agreed wholeheartedly with his insistence that the institute should focus solely upon improving the writing of the expository and argumentative essay. But another sizable group argued strongly for personal writing and for giving students the freedom to write about whatever they wanted to write about. It was in this sharp division that I found the solution. Either the next day or the day after, I told the group of a major change I was making. We would divide the institute for the rest of the summer into two totally separate groups that could focus on their own interests, meeting in different rooms and coming together only for guest speakers and our weekly Thursday evening potluck dinners. The teachers were more than satisfied and, strangely enough, did not think this drastic solution odd. They even gave each other pet names: the Hard-Noses and the Touchy-Feelies.

The experiment of the two institutes in two different rooms might have satisfied the teachers, but once I set it up, I found it impossible. It simply was not true to the heart of the project. The project I had envisioned was about talented teachers coming together and sharing their expertise, respecting and learning from their varied approaches. It was not about choosing up sides about how or what to teach. At the end of the fourth week, I called a halt to this 1975 summer institute. It was tearing the model apart. I invited everyone to a backyard barbecue at my home with plenty of good food and drink—which seemed to give our time together that summer a happy ending.

Looking back, I understand that this disaster (at least it seemed so at the time) might have been avoided if we had had in place the interview process that by the third year had become a key element of the summer institute. But for the first two years, interviews were not part of our selection process. For our first institute, I invited many of the teachers I had worked with in one way or another and knew to be excellent, and those I had not known were recommended by colleagues I respected. The summer fellows the following year were selected in much the same way, but when that difficult institute was over, I knew from then on we would have a selection process with the final cut based on a personal interview. Ever since, we have used the interview to learn a great deal about each teacher, and to give teachers a chance to learn more about BAWP. We talk about the special nature of our teacher-centered project, and teachers talk about their approaches to teaching writing, telling us what they do and why they do it. But this experience during the second summer institute taught us we were not looking for only the "hotshots." We were looking for teachers who can respect and learn from their talented colleagues, who can accept our assumption that there is no single best way to teach writing. Initiating a selection process the third year turned out to be a major event in the refinement of the Bay Area Writing Project model.

A Year in the Life of the Writing Project

✍ *The Selection Process: No End to Talent* ✍

BY THE THIRD YEAR, the key elements of the writing project model were fully in place, and we were getting a picture of what a year's work would look like for us. It needed to begin with the invitational summer institute selection process. Early in the calendar year, we sent out a call for nominations. Primarily, we sought nominations from former summer fellows who knew the project. They recommended colleagues or sometimes teachers they'd heard about in other ways. For example, Kim Davis, chair of Subject A at UC Berkeley and a former summer institute fellow, had gone to a party where some friends raved to him about their daughter's fourth-grade teacher. The daughter was writing and writing and getting to be very good at it. So Kim called and told me about Ed Allen. We also phoned colleagues in teacher training programs in other Bay Area universities and colleges and asked them about outstanding teachers they knew through their work in the schools. I always felt comfortable with nominations if I knew who was doing the nominating, but in time I realized that was much too limiting, so we began to seek out nominations from districts where we had yet to be involved.

We sent application forms to the eighty or more teachers nominated each year, asking them such questions as, "What is your approach to teaching writing?" "What have you had most success with?" "What would you like to know more about?" "Have you had any previous experience with the writing project?" On occasion, we called those who did the nominating for more information. Each spring we hoped to identify forty or so teachers we would like to interview.

In the beginning, we had to learn how to interview. Frequently, I would be so excited talking to the teachers about the project that I'd eat up a good chunk of the hour. As one teacher left the room one spring, I remember turning to Mary K. Healy, who became our codirector, and asking her, half seriously, "Who was that?" I had to learn to keep my mouth shut. In time we discovered we needed to ask just two questions: "How do you teach writing?" and "Why do you do it that way?" And then we'd sit back and listen to the teachers talk themselves into or out of the institute. Many teachers frequently reached down to a sack full of the things they had brought along to show us, but we'd put them off for a bit. "Just talk to us for a while; we can look at what you've brought later."

Both questions were equally important. The "why" question was a tougher one for many teachers; some told us they'd never been asked this question before. The teachers who took off on the "why" question usually knew who they were as teachers. They were aware, thoughtful, and almost without exception, they were not teachers who used formulas, textbook exercises, or gimmickry. I can remember only one teacher who couldn't speak to either question. She was so nervous she couldn't make a sound. I excused her from the interview as quickly as I could. I had great empathy for her, realizing that if I had faced this challenging situation in my first years as a teacher I too might have been speechless.

In our interviews, we were looking for certain qualities. We wanted teachers who were both strong and open—that is, teachers who were confident about their own practices and at the same time interested in knowing what other teachers were doing. Beyond these personal qualities, we were looking for a good mix of elementary, secondary, and college teachers, men and women from various ethnic backgrounds, teachers from bilingual and ESL classrooms, and teachers from disciplines other than English who had made good use of writing in their teaching. Once BAWP became well established, we began inviting five former summer fellows to the institute, a practice that continues today. These teachers participate in all of the standard institute activities and take on numerous staff roles as well. They join the Monday noon staff meetings, help get the editing/response groups off to a good start, coach teachers with their demonstrations, and help with follow-up sessions. Their support adds tremendous strength to the institute.

When we interviewed teachers, we also, of course, looked for those who gave us some indication that they could be successful teachers of other teachers. In some cases we knew immediately. But for the most part, it was hard to tell until that year's institute had run its course. Teaching fellow teachers takes classroom teachers into a world far different from that of teaching their own students. Through the dynamics of the institute—the trial-run workshops, the interplay with other teachers, the reactions to ideas—we discovered much more about the teachers BAWP had brought together, but sometimes even then we really didn't know which teachers would become part of that corps of teachers who were successful working with other teachers.

From the first institute on, I noted that many of the teachers, strong and successful as I knew them to be, could also be shy, hesitant to put themselves forward, and uncomfortable when praised. Some of them also brought with them their own set of fears: fear of revealing themselves, fear of making a fool of themselves, fear of letting others see their writing, fear of speaking out.

In general, however, the Bay Area Writing Project over its twenty-six years has had no trouble identifying teachers for the summer institute. Indeed, the project's structure has become self-perpetuating: successful teachers teach other teachers how to become more successful through inservice workshops, and these teachers are later identified as candidates for the summer institute. I've heard other NWP directors describe this same phenomenon.

THE TEACHER AS ARTIST

When we seek out teachers for the summer institute, we look for exemplary teachers who know why they do what they do, but we also look for teachers who possess a heavy dose of imagination and creativity. When we find a teacher who mixes competence with fresh ideas, we know we probably have a teacher who can teach other teachers. Such a teacher is BAWP teacher-consultant Bob Alpert, as his account of his first teaching experience makes clear.

In the fall of 1968, at 3:10 P.M. on a Friday afternoon, I was hired in Albany to teach sixth grade. School had started the prior week, and I was recruited because of an unexpected increase in students. I can't remember the man's name who conducted the interview, but I vividly remember following behind him, up the stairs, down the hallway, and into room 12 at Cornell School. Room 12 was the storage room for the entire school district. There were worn wooden desks randomly stacked as if they were pieces of one of those children's puzzle games where the object is to move a piece from the pile without causing the whole thing to collapse. There were piles of books published by companies like Ginn. "We've hired two custodians to help you straighten this room tomorrow. Books and supplies were ordered, but won't arrive for a few weeks. A list of student names will be available in the office on Monday morning. Here's a key."

"Uh, . . . thanks," I mumbled.

On the way home, I took a slight detour, choosing to drive along the frontage road paralleling the San Francisco Bay on the Berkeley/Oakland border. I stopped and sat on some barnacle-encrusted rocks at the water's edge. It was obviously low tide because between where I was sitting and the waterline was an expanse of grayish brown mud with shallow pools left by receding water. The place stunk, probably because of a combination of rotting food and rubbish tossed by passing motorists and the natural decay of algae exposed to sunlight at low tide.

I was thinking that I should have listened to my parents and gone to law school. The thought of facing thirty-four sixth-grade students on Monday without the slightest notion of what I was going to teach was terrifying. In frustration, I kicked at a rock partially buried in the mud. Out scurried several small green crabs. One half-dollar-size specimen picked the edge of my shoe as its next hiding place. I carefully kneeled down without moving my foot to take a better look. The obtuse angle of the setting sunlight caused the crab to light up. She was blowing phosphorescent bubbles from her gill slits. I crouched in the mud absolutely transfixed. Each cell of that animal was illuminated in flame. I momentarily lost my breath . . . as if I had been jolted to consciousness. I knew then that if I could share this type of feeling with my students, I would be teaching them something worthwhile.

I spent the remaining few hours of dusk crawling around in the mud "seeing" crabs. Seeing has always been for me a higher and more intense level of looking or watching. Those green crabs had six hairy legs and two prominent symmetrical pinchers. They scudded sideways, always protecting their backs, while pivoting to watch with two steely eyes mounted on protruding stalks. I interpreted their behaviors as being defensive. How long had they inhabited this polluted environment with its magnificent view of the Golden Gate Bridge, yet so close to humans and traffic? Seeing was detailing what's on the surface while also interpreting what's implied under the surface. I had my theme for guided reading and writing. On Monday, I'd bring green crabs and the accompanying oozy mud into the classroom in dish tubs. We'd write personified crab stories, estimate and measure their scudding bursts, and stage interpretive crab dances to Dave Brubeck. On Wednesday, we'd take a field trip to the Berkeley Mud Flats. I wondered if the University of California library was open on Saturday. Was there any written material on green crabs? By the time I got back to my car it was 7:45 P.M. I had to crouch down behind my car to remove my muddy "going to an interview" new suit. It wasn't the first or last time I'd be in trouble for getting dirty before changing into my play clothes.

The Spring Meeting: Getting Comfortable

ANOTHER ASPECT OF THE INSTITUTE that we established early on and that continues today is the Spring Meeting. In late May or early June, the new summer fellows meet for the first time at a Saturday meeting and luncheon at the UC Berkeley Faculty Club. The meeting starts with the teachers introducing themselves, and if any are shy about mentioning highlights in their careers—being named Oakland's Teacher of the Year, or having an article accepted for publication in *National Geographic,* or working as scriptwriter for Lucasfilm, or serving as mentor teacher for their district—we make sure such things are said.

During this meeting, we talk again about the writing project and its model and describe as carefully as possible everything that will be expected of the teachers during the five weeks of the institute. The teachers will be called on to

- demonstrate a particular practice or approach they have had success with as teachers of writing

- write four major pieces: sometimes, in the beginning, we asked that the first three be on a single topic of their choice and that they treat this topic with three distinct approaches, that is, a re-creation of an experience, a personal essay, and a poem or play; the fourth paper would be on writing (a personal position paper, an article, or a writing policy statement for their school or department)

- meet three afternoons each week with three or four other teachers in a writing group

- read books, articles, and research mostly of their own choosing in the literature of their field.

Now, as then, the teachers are reminded that the first draft of their first paper, with four additional copies for their writing group, will be due on the first day of the institute.

About this time, many of the new arrivals are getting nervous wondering what they have gotten themselves into. The new arrivals are not sure what they are doing in the company of all these great teachers. To reassure them, BAWP invites a few former summer fellows to the meeting to talk about their experiences during their summer institutes—their demonstrations, their writing, and their work with their editing/response groups. They are fellow classroom teachers and therefore believable. Our guests blunt most of this newcomer stage fright as they talk and laugh about their mishaps and their many joys during the institute, so that our new fellows realize how important the writing project has become to other classroom teachers like themselves.

Early on, I believed it was very important that our new fellows plunged in and wrote on this occasion, and this is something we still do. Sometimes I asked Liz Simons, a folklorist with a special interest in names, to lead the group in writing a short piece on the topic: "What story can you tell about how you got your name?" I personally enjoyed expounding on this topic, deploring the shortness of my name—Jim Gray. The name can be said in less than a second. It has no weight or substance, communicating nothing at all. I envy Mozart with his lineup of distinguished names, or I wish that my first name could have been Maximillian or Sebastian. This exercise has generally produced positive results. By the afternoon session—when new summer fellows are assigned to their writing groups—they enthusiastically read the stories of their names to the three or four teachers they will be working with throughout the summer.

Finally, at the Spring Meeting teachers are presented with their stipend to cover the costs of fees, books, and incidental expenses. When I was director, I usually closed the meeting by telling the new participants that they would soon be able to add to their resumes two new accomplishments: summer fellow and teacher-consultant of the Bay Area Writing Project at UC Berkeley.

⌒ *The Summer Institute:* ⌒
The Preparation of a Teacher-Consultant

THE SUMMER INSTITUTE SCHEDULE came to consist of five weeks of four full days (9:00 A.M. to 3:30 P.M.), each with a three-day weekend. From the start, we expected our fellows to evolve individually and collectively as teachers and as writers during this time, and for this change to occur, we found we needed at least five weeks together. The four days, which frequently run past the targeted closing time, are packed and intense; the three-day weekend provides a time to rest, think, and write. Around the third or fourth week, the groups coalesce, and from that time, institute activities take place in an atmosphere of mutual trust that facilitates communal work. Over the years, some sites have felt the need to opt for a five-day, four-week schedule. They have had their reasons for this, but I believe that they miss something wonderful by cutting short the last portion of the institute when the group has established itself as a community of writers and teachers.

The years I was director of the Bay Area Writing Project, we scheduled the hours of 9:00 A.M. to 12:30 P.M. with two one-hour demonstrations, announcements, the reading of logs, and a short break. This schedule for a typical group of twenty-five teachers freed up time for the flexibility all institutes need. The writing groups, or editing/response groups, met three afternoons each week, and reading groups one afternoon.

ᗌ *Teacher Demonstrations* ᗌ

I HAVE A HARD TIME getting myself out of the habit of saying, "The heart of the writing project is . . ." and then coming to a full stop because I can think of so many "hearts"—all of them important. Still, for a teachers-teaching-teachers project, a good case can be made that the teacher demonstrations are a likely Number One Heart.

In the early days of BAWP, our demonstrations began on the second or third day of the first week. The first of these were presented by teachers we believed were closest to being ready to conduct workshops for other teachers. Some summer fellows, early on in the institute, were nervous about giving demonstrations; we tried to identify such people and schedule them later, so they would benefit from observing and participating in the demonstrations of others.

Over the years, I've observed hundreds of teachers demonstrate their approaches to teaching writing, and I remember so many that are worth describing. But I'll settle on two. Both teachers taught in elementary schools and in two quite different worlds. Pat Gregory taught a mixed class of third- and fourth-graders in an all African-American urban school in Oakland, and Ed Allen was a fourth-grade teacher in affluent Marin County.

Pat Gregory started teaching in the Philippines and later moved to British Columbia, where she taught Native Americans. When she joined the institute in 1979, she had been teaching for eight years in Prescott School in Oakland. She told us that throughout her long career she had never had a white student in any of her classes.

The major outside source for Pat's ideas came from a dog-eared copy of Sylvia Ashton-Warner's book *Teacher*. Pat worked to create a language-rich environment in her classroom in much the same way as Sylvia Ashton-Warner had done in teaching her Maori students. Word lists were pinned up all around her room.

Pat began her demonstration by telling us that at the beginning of the year some of her students had a very difficult time writing. To demonstrate how slow some students were in getting their words down, she went to the board and wrote a list of the letters in the alphabet in one column, and then she put a random number after each letter. Then she turned to us and told us to write a short sentence using numbers for the letters. Our heads went up then down, up then down, up then down—all of that for the word "The."

Pat told her students, "If you're good boys and girls in the morning, you'll get to write in the afternoon." Writing was something special in Pat's class, a treat, a happy occasion in the school day. In the afternoons, Pat's students wrote in two different journals that they kept in the room. In the first, each student wrote about real incidents from daily life, about a family visit to Aunt Lumpy's, about how they missed a brother who was no longer living at home, about having a lunch bag stolen at recess, about a weekend trip to an amusement part. In the second journal, they wrote about what they had been studying in the morning and what they had learned. Pat's students kept daily learning logs about what they remembered about planets, electricity, American Indians, the human body, black history, and so on. Pat had never heard about writing across the curriculum, yet she knew the power writing had in promoting real learning. Pat brought samples of student journals for us to read to demonstrate what her students were able to do. It was a rich collection. One student wrote the following piece after seeing another class put on a play about Harriet Tubman and after memorizing a poem about her. The student correctly worked lines from that poem into her own piece (those lines appear in italics below).

Yesterday we took a walk through Black History. I learned about Harriet Tubman. *She didn't take no stuff. And wasn't scared of nothing neither.* All of the white people beat her and *slaved* her. And made her do all the work. She was beat with sticks and everything else. But one hot night she ran for her freedom with the slave catchers right behind her. But she kept on going till she got to the north where the catchers couldn't find her. And she ran for her freedom nineteen times to save black sisters and brothers. Harriet Tubman *didn't take no stuff,* wasn't scared of nothing neither. *Didn't come in this world to be no slave, and didn't stay one either.*

—*Sharon, Grade 3*

Ed Allen began his workshop with a demonstration of what he says to his fourth-graders on the opening day of class:

If any of you can say "yes" to any of the following questions, please raise your hand:

How many of you have been kidnapped by pirates in the Caribbean and taken to a Pirate's Cove and held for ransom? How many of you have that experience in your background? If you do, raise your hands now. *Questioning looks on their faces. No hands up.*

How many of you have gone to Cape Kennedy, stolen a rocket, and gone to the moon? Have any of you ever done that? *Amused chuckles. No hands up.*

How many of you have been attacked by aliens on the way to school? Has that happened to any of you?

No? None of you have ever had any of these experiences? Well then, we won't write about such things!

How many of you have sometimes not wanted to get up out of your warm beds in the morning to go to school? *Students don't know whether to raise hands or not. A few tentatively raised.*

How many of you have said something to a friend that you wish you had never said? *Hands begin to go up.*

How many of you have been alone in the dark in a strange place and felt nervous? *Hands up.*

How many of you have hurt your mother's feelings and felt terrible about it afterward? *Hands all up.*

That's the stuff we'll write about in this class, our clearly remembered moments of experience.

~

The heart of Ed's workshop was his demonstration of how he taught students to write what he called "The Short Piece," a single, sharply focused incident from real experience:

She started walking slowly down the steps of the old yellow bus, the brisk wind coming closer to catching up with her. A big fifth grader pushed her down the rest of the way. She clumsily fell into a rushing stream of water from the many days it had rained. The water slowly oozed its way through her shoes and into her socks. Her whole foot suddenly froze as she walked on, water whooshing from one side of her shoe to another. Her eyes were full of hatred for the bully fifth grader who had shoved her into the cold, frosty winter day. The cool gray sky above her stood out, fog surrounding everything. Mount Tam on one side of her stood big and bold with its rough, pleasing look. She turned into her street and blew light puffs of smoke from her mouth and watched it dissolve into the bitter, cold air. She moved slowly and took her icy cold hands out of her pockets and reached for the key to open the old, black garage door. It opened with a jerk, and she walked into the house. The warm air made her wish she was back outside.   —*Laura, Grade 4*

The short pieces, Ed explained, were written in drafts, with students responding to one another's work in pairs and small groups, with Ed also responding as he moved about the room. Students wrote scores of these pieces throughout the year, and much of what was written was published, either reproduced and collected in thematic anthologies, such as the *We Love Our Mommies* collection the students prepared for Mother's Day, or, on occasion, printed on Ed's classroom printing press (in the precomputer age) in stylishly designed publications. Because most student work was published and written for real audiences, even if it was simply put up on bulletin boards in the classroom or in the school halls, these young authors took great care that the final versions were correct and accurate. During Ed's trial-run workshop, we wrote our own short pieces and read numerous pieces Ed's fourth-graders had written.

Pat and Ed were among those teachers who grasped intuitively the process of demonstrating successful practice to other teachers. Other summer institute participants had a rockier time. It occurred to us that many fellows needed more help than they were getting.

⇜ *Coaching* ⇝

EARLY ON, WE BEGAN COACHING the fellows before their demonstrations, and as a result, the overall quality of the demonstrations improved immeasurably. After a few summer institutes, we realized we were learning some things about successful teacher demonstrations, and we decided to share what we knew rather than set our fellows free to learn entirely from their own mistakes. In fact, some teachers had never done anything like this before. During the coaching sessions, directors and former fellows listened to what the teachers were planning for their demonstrations. I would listen for what I learned were the most successful elements: Is it focused on one idea or approach? How will the audience be involved? Will there be time for discussion? Will it be clear to the audience why the teacher is demonstrating this particular practice? Before coaching, teachers frequently tried to do too much, or spent too much time introducing what they were going to do, or left little time for involvement or discussion. All of these problems could be anticipated in a coaching session and nipped in the bud.

Looking back now, I realize how unfair it was during the first summer institutes, before we instituted coaching, to ask teachers to give an exemplary demonstration when they had little understanding of what was expected. For example, coaching would have helped the teacher who gave a lecture on English sentence patterns culled from several different textbooks, which contradicted one another. For her demonstration, the teacher put together a handout of all the twenty-three basic sentence patterns she had found in the texts, then she read and described them to us one by one. After this lecture, the teachers sat stupefied in their chairs: not one question was asked, not one comment was raised. Teachers who have knowledge of sentence patterns are well positioned to help their students as they struggle with sentences, but these teachers learned little about the subject that day. Because we had not coached the teacher, an opportunity was squandered.

⌒

Today, the entire process of the demonstrations—planning and conducting a trial-run workshop, and observing, evaluating, and participating in other teachers' workshops—begins to prepare fellows to become writing project teacher-consultants. For the BAWP staff, the demonstrations help identify the teacher-consultants who are ready to conduct workshops in the schools. Those who conduct excellent workshops are put to work as soon as possible in the follow-up school-year programs. Others are worked in more gradually after they've had time and opportunity to sharpen their presentations. BAWP also holds monthly Saturday meetings open to the public that give teachers the opportunity to become comfortable as presenters.

But from the start, we wanted to give teachers other opportunities to work with their colleagues in the project, since we knew that highly successful teachers of young people could feel uneasy or ill prepared to teach teachers. Some teachers would never be used, and some would opt out on their own when they discovered that they just didn't like giving workshops.

One thing I learned early on while watching teachers demonstrate their best practices to other teachers was how much these already successful teachers could learn from one another. Initially, I thought only of preparing these teachers to teach others and gave little thought to how much they too wanted to learn how to be better teachers. In the institute, even our strongest teachers seemed to realize they had a grasp on only a piece of what was known about the teaching of writing. In the large and expanding field of written composition, they taught specific things very well indeed, but in the summer institute, they learned more and stretched their abilities, both through their summer institute reading and by participating in the demonstrations of other teachers, who showed them new skills and approaches to teaching writing.

Another important point needs to be made about the nature of the demonstrations. Institute teachers themselves determine the content of their workshops. I would tell them to pick their best shot. This freedom has important implications for the way the writing project works. By allowing excellent teachers the opportunity to demonstrate their best practices without restrictions, the project remains open to new ideas, approaches, and variations. This open mindset keeps us from ever saying, "This is it! *This* is the Bay Area Writing Project approach to the teaching of writing!" The writing project is not a writing curriculum or even a collection of best strategies; it is a structure that makes it possible for exemplary teachers to share with other teachers ideas that work.

Yet at the same time, over the lifetime of the project, certain ideas and approaches have risen to the top like cream in an old-fashioned milk bottle: the importance of teaching writing as a process, the importance of paying attention to all stages within that process, the ways in which writing can promote learning, the need to have students experience a wide range of writing experiences, the need to begin writing instruction in the early primary grades and to keep attending to it throughout schooling. While these are some of the ideas project teachers promote—ideas that at times are identified with the project, locally and nationwide—the writing project has always remained open to whatever approaches work, from whatever source. The net will continue to be cast.

Above all, the writing project honors teacher knowledge, knowledge that can come only from the practice of teaching writing. When classroom teachers are respected and recognized for what they know, when they are treated as the experts they are, they gain strength and become less defensive and more open. Such an atmosphere of trust encourages honest dialogue and a breaking down of traditional barriers between universities and schools, and as a result, teachers from both settings can begin working together as mutually respected colleagues.

∽ *Teachers Writing* ∽

FROM THE BEGINNING, the summer institute has had a writing component, but I didn't realize its central importance until we started getting feedback from the teachers. During the early institutes, I was so focused on what I thought was the main goal—putting classroom teachers at the center of things, preparing them to teach other teachers, tapping and celebrating the knowledge from practice that only they had—that I was surprised and a bit bewildered when they would rate their own experience with writing as the most important part of the summer institute. In their last-day evaluations, they would say such things as, "I loved every bit of what we did this summer, but it was the writing that will have the most lasting effect on me and on my teaching."

Both components—teacher demonstrations and writing—are essential to the institute. But if we only emphasized the need for writing teachers to write, the Bay Area Writing Project would still be an important program. Given the chance to spend the summer writing, freed from the heavy load of teaching, free to write about whatever topic they want, and helped and guided by their writing group peers, teachers become writers. They rise to a new level: when they leave the institute they're teachers of writing *who are also writers*. They have experienced writing as a process. We'd get comments like, "I always thought I knew what revision meant until this summer. *Now* I know what revision means!" and, "I've learned more about the teaching of writing than I've ever known before, and I learned most through the writing I did."

Though teachers are given freedom to write what they choose, we do suggest a structure that includes four major pieces of writing, the first three on a topic of personal choice with no two pieces alike, an assignment that typically moves the writer from a personal experience to an essay about some idea inherent in the initial experience. This assignment invites experimentation in genre and point of view and guarantees the writer a varied writing experience, and as such it serves as a model for student writers as well. The fourth and final assignment could be either a policy statement on the teaching of writing that expresses the teacher's current thinking, an article on teaching writing to be submitted for publication, or a working draft of a school writing policy that could be presented to colleagues for their reactions and contributions. We make the important point that these four key pieces should be written in privacy outside of the institute.

I soon learned that the best way to make clear the kinds of writing that would be expected of fellows was to tell stories of what former summer fellows had written.

Fred Zook, for his first paper, wrote several different short descriptive pieces about the small town in Kansas that he left when he moved to California—particular places that were strong in Fred's memory: a main street cafe, a filling station, a family farm. His second piece was a re-creation of two letters he remembered seeing as a boy that had been written by a great aunt describing what Kansas was like when it was still a territory. Fred re-created these letters, writing with an old-fashioned pen in an old-fashioned script and then putting them in the oven until they were crinkly tan. His third piece was a one-act play about a farmer, who was now a wealthy landowner, and his wife reminiscing about what their lives had been like when they both lived on small family farms (Fred and another fellow put on Fred's play à la Readers' Theater on the last day of the institute). Fred's final piece that summer (we started with four pieces on one topic in the early years) was a personal essay on the growth and changes in agriculture in the United States during his lifetime.

My wife, Stephanie, was a high school teacher in the 1970s and joined the summer institute. The story of how she moved a piece of her writing from one genre to another illustrates how members of a response group help one another through the process. Stephanie's brother John served two tours in Vietnam, unscathed, then came home to join the Pinole, California, police force. During his first week on the force, he and his partner were called to a local bar where an old man who had drunk too much had taken out his gun and was waving it about. John went into the bar through the back door; his partner came through the front. The instant the drunk saw John, he shot and killed him.

Stephanie wrote first about what it was like when she arrived at her sister-in-law's home early the next morning after the killing. Stephanie's mother was already there, sitting quietly in the front room. There were a number of police in the room, but no one was talking. The only sound Stephanie heard was the familiar squeak of leather on leather from the holsters and heavy belts of the police. Mary, John's wife, was in the kitchen, and her young son, Tom, was still sleeping. When the boy woke up and came into the kitchen, Mary told him: "Tom, something bad has happened to your daddy. A man shot him, and you're daddy is dead." Tom looked at his mother and then ran to the sink, where he threw up.

Stephanie's powerful piece captured the silence of grief in that home. In addition to comments on her craft, two members of her writing group had similar stories to tell: Bob Hogan, executive director of NCTE and a member of the institute that year, told the story of his brother, who was shot and killed by a sniper who was shooting at cars from a hill bordering a freeway. Jerry Herman, another member of the writing group, told a story about his neighbor, who heard a noise in his house in the middle of the night and shot and killed his own young daughter as she was coming up the stairway. After hearing these tales, Stephanie had found the subject of the essay she was to write next. She took these two stories and combined them with her story and wrote an essay that pleaded the case for gun control. With the help of her response group, she was able to move from experience to idea in two separate pieces around the same content.

But in addition to pieces growing out of their lives, we also wanted our fellows to reflect on their work, particularly in light of their experiences during the previous five weeks in the institute. How had this encounter changed the way they taught? A teacher who once had students keep journals, only because her department head encouraged it, now explained how she developed a rationale for this strategy. Another teacher challenged the value of unfocused free writing and laid out a strategy for prewriting that involved a combination of openness and structure. We came to call this assignment a position paper.

BAWP fellow and Phillips Exeter Academy faculty member Norv Rindfleisch turned his position paper into a writing policy statement for his school. Here is an excerpt from Norv's statement, which reflects some of the ideas he encountered during his summer in the institute.

Writing is composing, and composing is a decision making process of great complexity even on the simplest level. It is more than grammar or spelling or punctuation. It is above all a process of thinking, feeling, ordering, organizing. It entails an inner sense of revision, a mysterious power in all students that continues to amaze teachers of writing who permit and encourage it to operate. Writing is also a process of discovery, a mode of knowing. Students often find out what they really know by being forced to write; ideally they do not understand any content until they have written it. It is then, after a first draft, after the writer discovers what he really wants to say, that the shaping toward form and correctness begins.

WRITING TEACHERS WRITE

Because teachers of writing need to write, writing is an integral part of our summer institutes. But as Kim Stafford, director of the Oregon Writing Project at Lewis and Clark, points out, for many the dictate that summer fellows write is not just one more requirement—it is the very charm that has lured some teachers into turning over to the writing project five weeks of their summer vacation.

I suspect that every site director is familiar with a ritual I have experienced often while interviewing teachers for participation in the writing project. I ask, "What are you so curious about that you want to give up a month of your summer to join us?" In reply, they often say something about teaching first: "I want to be a better teacher." "I want to learn how to use more writing in my teaching." Or, "Friends who have gone through the writing project seem to have a new teaching energy, and I want that . . . ." But then, often in hushed tones, as if to confess a great secret, this same applicant will also say: "I want to get back to my own writing." "I need to put down some stories I have been carrying." "My grandmother has died, and I want to remember." Or, "I have to see what happens when I try to do what I tell my students to do—I want to write!" These teachers, lured into the chance to spend time writing together, know the great secret: a writer is the opposite of a piece of chalk—the more you write, the bigger you become.

Just as these teachers are more interested in what their own students can do than what they can absorb, these teachers want to know how they can express, discover, and surprise themselves by writing. They went into teaching because they loved to read and to write, and now they find themselves with precious little time to do either. The summer institute is a time to return to first love.

As a high school student once told me, "I write in order to learn what I might see beyond the wall of a first glance." In my experience, teachers who choose to enter the writing project in order to write have discovered a similar need. They need to see beyond the restrictions of their own educations. They need to unlearn certain things about the nature of authority, by returning to their own artesian source of understanding: thoughtful recollection through writing. We often start with personal writing—the poem, the impassioned editorial, the fragment of memoir—in order to be utterly clear about the location of authority in the writing. In school, and especially in graduate school, we have all written under conditions where the teacher knew more about the subject than the writer did. When this is the case, the writing is a test, not true exposition of original insight. So in the writing project, we often begin with personal writing (your research has been your life), and then advance toward more objective forms.

We start with poems and stories where the writer is the only one who knows: What is your earliest memory? When did you first encounter the natural world? What happened at the dinner table in childhood? Tell a moment from your own experience as a student in the grade you are teaching now: a time you got in big trouble, a mysterious relative, the darkest night, learning to drive . . . to kiss . . . to fail . . . to be silent.

And even when we have begun to write essays, articles, and teacher research, it may still be true that the most important writing we do for professional growth is our personal writing. We may publish our findings for others, but we may learn the most ourselves from the freewrite, the journal, the letter to a friend. For our students are making writing, but we are making writers. And when we do our own writing, we are making learners of ourselves, in the fluid process of insight as it unfolds.

Sometimes we have argued about the relative merits of personal and expository writing practice. Sometimes we have accused personal writing of being "just therapy," or accused thinly expository writing of being "cold." I don't want to choose. I see these two as good hands, left and right, and their proper use in the ambidextrous work of a writer true to both passion and clarity. The writing will show and the writer will know when it is time to turn from one hand to the other, and back again.

I am a bigger soul for the writing I have done in the company of my writing project colleagues. I am a more deeply informed teacher for the writing I have witnessed as it came into being during the fifteen summer institutes it has been my privilege to witness. And I know I am a fortunate learner, stunned by wonder as I bow over the alchemy of words, staring into the page where I am invented again and again. A writer, I am alone there, and in good company. I float on my back, stay calm, and breathe.

~

TEACHERS AS RESEARCHERS

If the writing project believes that teacher knowledge is a key to better schools, how do we formalize and disseminate what teachers know? Part of our answer has been teacher research. Here, Marian Mohr, codirector of the Northern Virginia Writing Project and a leader in teacher research, describes how she became a teacher-researcher and how she establishes the connection between teacher research and the work of the National Writing Project.

Teacher research began, in my own thinking, during the first summer institute of the Northern Virginia Writing Project in 1978. When I tried to order my thoughts as the weeks steamed by, I found two parallel directions. One: There was much yet to be learned about writing, teaching, and learning. The other: Although a classroom teacher, I could contribute to that learning. Both thoughts amazed me.

The first direction came from my surprise that in this mix of very professional people with obvious skills at all grade levels, there was no consensus on how to teach writing. Trying to steer clear of blaming one another, we were without generalizations. We told our individual teaching stories and nodded to one another. We wanted to try out one another's lessons, and we talked about writing process, but we neither received nor transmitted a recommended way to teach.

I also saw that in the theory and research world we heard and read about, most theorists and researchers didn't know what practitioners knew. Because

I was a classroom teacher, I was in a position to find out what I needed to know by asking questions of my students and keeping track of what happened as I taught. I might find out things that would be useful to other teachers and perhaps even to that world of theory and research outside the classroom.

This new understanding was emancipating. Although I had been in teacher meetings where my dedication had been vaguely lauded, I knew that I was not a participant in the important professional conversations about teaching and learning. I was given curriculum to teach, assigned textbooks written and chosen by others, and told how to manage my students. In meetings attended and memos received, it was made painfully clear that I was not trusted to do my job. By the time of the writing project summer institute, I was experienced enough to brag about undermining official edicts, closing my door, and really teaching. Hiding out seemed sensible, not defensive.

But that summer, I saw a way into the profession. I would teach, whatever the constraints, ask my students questions I didn't know the answers to, and write about what we learned together. In September, I retitled my teaching journal "Research Log" and began looking closely at the revision processes of my students and writing about what I saw happening.

I was joined by others. Anne, a high school English teacher, had done her masters thesis by enrolling in a high school chemistry class and writing to learn the material. Mary was looking at struggling writers in primary grades and observing how they learned to write and, along with writing, to read. Other teacher-consultants joined us. Patty Sue Williams, another primary grades teacher, was also looking at beginning writing. Bernie Glaze was trying out writing-to-learn with her history students. Marion MacLean was interested in how her students thought about and evaluated their writing. We began meeting on a regular basis to talk about what we were learning, and we invited other interested teacher-consultants to join us.

At the base of teacher research was something we did every day as classroom teachers—observing how our students learned and how our teaching interacted with their learning. Teacher research involved intention and attention. It involved writing about my teaching and being honest about doubts and failures as well as about what seemed to be successes. It involved a new kind of distance from my students—viewing their words and actions as data. But the more I was able to see my students as part of my research, the closer I came to understanding how they learned and the closer we became as a group intent on learning.

With the present spotlight on school reform, teacher research takes on special importance. Schools are being restructured to give teachers a voice in decision making. The knowledge base for this decision making can be our research. Suppose a school's test scores are seen as too low. Teacher-researchers can investigate why the scores are low and how to teach so that students learn more. As contributors to knowledge, teachers then need not be defensive victims.

Teacher research and writing projects were an especially good match. Like the writing project, teacher research is about teachers helping their colleagues and themselves; teacher research offers teacher-generated information about teaching and learning—colleague to colleague. Teachers who conduct research change their teaching in important ways and see the process as self-chosen, self-designed professional development.

Further, the writing project insists that teachers write. Teacher-researchers, as they revise their research reports, understand in their bones what writing-to-learn is all about and see writing as a help to their thinking. Their colleagues benefit as teacher-researchers give presentations and publish their work, expectations also fostered by writing projects. Writing projects are able to offer teacher-researchers the support—collegial if not always financial—to continue. A small writing project meeting of teachers where teachers are able to discuss their work in an atmosphere of trust that encourages them to speak freely and think deeply is worth a barrel of stipends.

Finally, just as ideas about the writing process and professional development moved from writing projects into individual schools and the profession as a whole, so did teacher research. Over the years, the writing project has offered important lessons in understanding how a grass-roots organization develops and prospers. Teacher research, growing within the organization, was able to benefit from the lessons, to stay close to the source—teaching and learning in classrooms.

〜 *Editing/Response Groups* 〜

THE WRITING RESPONSE GROUPS have always been the solid links in the chain that makes up the durable community of the summer institute. BAWP tries to have the writing groups in place by the Spring Meeting. In each group, we attempt a cross section of grade levels and ethnic and gender diversity. When I was director, on the afternoon of the first day just before the editing/response groups would meet for the first time, I would talk a bit about the ways these groups might work. I suggested one member read his or her first draft aloud after passing out copies so that the others could follow along. I urged group members not to jump in too quickly with comments or questions, allowing for thoughtful silence. I suggested that the writer begin the discussion, commenting on his or her intention. By encouraging writers to initiate this kind of global comment on their work, those who had not written much in recent years would not be able to merely sit back and listen to what others had to say. Conversely, those teachers who had done more writing and were more aggressive would not be able to micromanage the discussion.

In time, each group would find its own way to proceed, but I cautioned them to work for that crucial balance between praise and criticism as they became editors of one anothers' work. I told them how, in the first years of the project, some groups were overly supportive, and members felt short-changed when they found out that other groups had improved pieces by being responsibly critical.

I remember several first-year problems. The response groups became like families within the summer institute community, and like families, some groups functioned better than others. A typical difficulty: One member wants to be the teacher, taking charge and making arbitrary and sometimes quirky decisions for the group, rather than recognizing that all members of the group are there because they are accomplished teachers of writing. A participant in one of the early institutes announced to her group at its first meeting, "Writing is not oral interpretation. Writing is meant to be read silently. So, in this group we will not be reading our papers aloud to one another!" When we got wind of such heavy-handed behavior, we could usually end it by reminding institute participants that some fellows were not "more equal than others."

I was pleased the teachers took me at my word when I said that the afternoons were theirs to plan as they wished. Even with three full afternoons a week in writing groups, some groups always decided they needed more time, meeting for additional hours beneath the shade of the immense, old Italian stone pines just outside our building, or walking up the hill to the North Gate, sitting around outdoor picnic tables at La Val's restaurant or some other spot, and eating sandwiches and drinking beer as they read and talked about their work. They could go home early if they finished, or go home late if they hadn't. The only rules: "Give all writers the response time they need, and when a piece is complete, give me a copy to read."

As I began to receive drafts from the fellows, my responses followed a pattern that should by now be predictable. Just as a classroom teacher, early in the semester, is often disappointed by the first papers from students who have done little writing, I was disappointed by the fellows' early output, forgetting how rusty or inexperienced many of them were as writers. I said to myself, "I always knew it was bound to happen. We can't expect every group to have the kind of writers we've had in past summers." But then I'd find a piece with the beginnings of a glow, and I'd invite the writer to sit in the authors' chair—an idea we picked up from the strategies of elementary teachers—and read his or her piece to the group. The response and discussion would always be enthusiastic. I knew I would be able to continue to identify strong pieces for the authors' chair and that the general quality of the writing would improve. The BAWP directors who followed me ran the authors' chair more democratically, asking for volunteers. But our goal was the same: to spotlight excellence. Excellence—as long as everyone was given a fair shot at achieving it—inspired excellence both in our classrooms and in the summer institute.

Each summer the project published an anthology—with titles like "Much Ado About Writing," "Writing at Bay," or "Life Sentences"—containing the best of the fellows' work for distribution on the last day of the institute, which was also a day of celebration. The authors' chair got heavy use. The atmosphere was one of joy over the quality of the writing and appreciation for all the help these writers had received from one another. So special was this experience, some groups continued to meet after the institute was over.

⤳ *Readings and Research* ⤳

BECAUSE THE WRITING PROJECT has spotlighted the importance of teacher knowledge, hard-won through classroom experience, those looking at us from the outside have sometimes been left with the false impression that we are dismissive of theoretical ideas and academic research in writing. In fact, a portion of summer institute programs has always been devoted to the exploration of theory and research. As professionals, teachers need to immerse themselves in the *why* as well as the *what* of their work. Indeed, I have long had a vision that with the growth of more and more National Writing Project sites and with the growth of more subject-matter projects based on the writing project model, all of the nation's classrooms will eventually be staffed by successful and fully informed teacher-scholars. During the summer institutes, BAWP works to maintain a balance between knowledge gained through practice and knowledge gleaned through research and literature in the field. As teachers prepare for their demonstrations, they are asked to describe not only what they do but why they do it. They will often refer to books and articles that have influenced their teaching of writing as well as what they have learned from their classroom practice.

During the institute, one afternoon each week teachers come together in reading groups to discuss the articles and books on writing they have been reading. In recent years, the problem has been an embarrassment of riches. When Mary Ann Smith was director of BAWP, she organized these discussion groups by grade level: teachers read articles in one of their particular areas of interest and then picked one article high in interest and readability for all of the other teachers in the group to read, a winnowing process that resulted in lively discussions of some seminal pieces.

We do not expect, during the agenda-packed summer institute, to make teachers mavens in writing theory and research. Our goal is to whet their appetite for this knowledge, which can enrich their classroom practice. In many cases, as teachers learn more about theory and research, they realize that practices they have come to through classroom experience have foundations supported by academics and researchers, whose job it is to investigate how writing can best be taught. Many summer fellows have maintained the habit of reading research long after their summer institute has ended. This fact is evidenced by the growing number of articles melding classroom expertise and theoretical knowledge published in *The Quarterly*, NWP's journal of professional writing.

THINGS AREN'T LIKE THEY USED TO BE

"The writing project changed my life." We hear this regularly, a common assessment of a writing project summer.

The speaker in cases like this does not specify "professional life," which is as much as we are willing to take credit for. These paragraphs excerpted from Jane Juska's "Earthquake, or How I Stopped Worrying and Learned to Love the Bay Area Writing Project" tell the before-and-after writing project stories of one teacher-consultant.

BEFORE

For twenty of my thirty-four teaching years, the teaching of writing was beneath me, for I was a teacher of literature. My calling was to teach the best that had been thought and written to the most people. Writing was something the teacher assigned to students so that they could prove to the teacher that they knew what the teacher had said about the literature the teacher had assigned to be read. At its best, writing was the handmaiden to literature; at its worst, it looked like what my students turned in for me to attack with my red pencil.

I didn't expect kids to like my assignments; learning was hard work, and if they didn't believe me, just try to write one of the essays I assigned. Assignments went like this: "Read the two short stories in your anthology.

(See board for page numbers.) Compare and contrast the endings with the end in view of showing the *Weltanschauungen* of the two writers. Due tomorrow." I would spend the rest of the period explaining *Weltanschauungen*. Next day, there they'd be, rough drafts in hand—or not. Now what. I would show them what a final draft was to look like. I drew a sheet of blank paper on the board and a line on either side two inches from the edge of the paper. "Two inch margins on each side of the paper," I warned. "Deadline, hmmm,"—oh, the power!—"Friday." Oh thank god, they thought, two days to get their comparison/contrast into perfect shape. On Friday, here they came, final drafts in ink, and late Sunday night or, more likely, two weeks from that Sunday night, I would write at the end of the papers I had bludgeoned into submission something like, "If spelling is beyond you, perhaps margins are not. C-." "Don't you ever give A's?" they wanted to know. And then they went out into the hall where I had placed the classroom trash can so I would not have to watch them play basketball with their returned papers.

AFTER

The biggest change inside my classroom was that I wrote with the kids. Reform happens in the classroom, said Jim. Indeed, if we wait for the department or the school or the district or the state to make things better, change can take forever, maybe never, and if it does occur, it may not be to our liking. (See current state of affairs.) Reform in my classroom meant changing what went on between my kids and me. Writing is a great leveler. When I began writing with my students, the walls came down, the barriers collapsed, though that's not necessarily what I intended. No matter, the kids could see that, as a writer, I was as vulnerable as they, that I needed their response and advice as much as they needed mine. We became writers together. "What do you think of this?" I would ask when I brought my first paragraph of their assignment in for their help. I threw study questions out the window: we wrote our own. We exchanged a steady diet of literary analysis for a variety of ways of writing and thinking about a piece of literature; we made up our own topics. I quit making up tests; we all did it. We wrote before discussion and after. We wrote tons of first drafts, chose a couple, and worked hard to revise them into something we could put on the wall. We were all in this together. We liked it that way.

Because of the Bay Area Writing Project, I wrote all the time, everywhere I went, the movies, restaurants, the teachers' lounge. I filled journal upon journal with the uncertainty I felt still and always about my classroom teaching. I wrote endlessly about, How was I going to last the rest of the year with my fifth-period class in such chaos? I designed new and delicious tortures for any administrator who crossed me. I wrote about money, about summer, about sex, about the checker at the grocery store, and all my kids in first period and second and all the rest. They loved it when I read what I had written about them: "Shut up, she's going to read about us." Out of my logs came longer pieces; some got published, some not. Almost always, I wrote my way into clarity, into an understanding, into a lifting of the mists. I wrote my way into thinking, into a confidence that I could find a way through almost anything; and if I just wrote long enough, I came to know that I would find out something that I didn't know I knew. What a gift this writing. My students saw me writing; sometimes, I would stop in the middle of a class discussion and say, "Excuse me, that is so interesting I have to write it down." I would turn around to my journal on my desk and listen as the kids wondered while I wrote. Writing for me was nothing less than a miracle. And forever after, I have tried to make it happen for my students.

THE SUMMER INSTITUTE
BACK IN THE CLASSROOM

It's an unfortunate axiom that most of what passes for teacher "staff development" ends when the mandatory meeting is adjourned at 5:00 P.M. This is not the case with writing project workshops. Because writing project presentations are the work of teachers, the nuts and bolts of their demonstrations have a credibility that propels their work into classrooms. Yet the writing project experience affects classrooms in larger ways, as Sheridan Blau, director of California's South Coast Writing Project, explains.

Having experienced what it means to learn in a community of learners, teachers are inclined to count such learning as more authoritative and authentic than any other and to think of such learning as the proper aim of instruction. They therefore become determined to turn their own classrooms into learning communities that will function like a writing project, where respect for the intelligence of every learner is the starting place for all activity, and where all learners are expected and required to take responsibility for their own learning as well as for assisting others to learn—a community where learning entails the production of knowledge as well as its reception, and where knowledge is always seen as provisional and subject to challenge and refinement.

If that description sounds like everybody's definition of a model classroom, it is surely not every student's experience of classroom learning. In fact, I assume—with good reason, I believe—that few of us have had any sustained experience of learning in such a community during our years as students in classrooms and that all of us know something of how difficult it must be to translate such an ideal for a classroom into the classrooms we actually inhabit in schools. Classrooms do not typically include twenty to twenty-five students carefully selected as exemplary teachers and learners, as is the case in the summer institute, and they do not consist of adults whose professional lives have committed them to solving the very problems that define the curriculum.

Still, it is true that all good teachers find some ways to foster authentic and engaged learning in their classrooms some of the time. And the surest methods or strategies or programs for instruction that are most likely, most often, to produce such learning are usually those that fellows of a writing project site demonstrate to one another and to their colleagues in inservice programs. More important than these strategies and programs of instruction, however, the writing project provides an experience for teachers in a model community of learners, a model that works so well for most of the teachers who experience it that they spend the rest of their professional lives trying to create some version of it in their classrooms, where the conditions of membership and daily life do not usually conspire to help them.

A cynic might say that the writing project is so unlike a classroom that the experience it provides has no relevance to the life world of the school. But good teachers are not cynics—at least not about their teaching. It is a standing joke among writing project teachers, many of whom are veterans of thirty or more years of teaching, that we continue to teach every year with equal anticipation because we are hoping to finally get it right. Which does not for a moment imply that for thirty years we have gotten it wrong. Rather it speaks to our recognition of the difficulty that teaching presents to every teacher who continues to care about students and of the challenges that each student and classroom present to us anew.

Teacher Evaluation of the Summer Institute

We learned early on that if our goal in doing an end-of-institute evaluation is to get information to improve a generally successful program, then an evaluation form consisting merely of number rankings won't work. If the respondents felt good about the experience, as almost all did, and were asked to rank aspects of the program from low to high, one to six, we could expect very few responses below five and a lot of sixes and sevens, with happy faces drawn in the margins.

We discarded our initial form. Instead, we asked the teachers during the last morning of the summer institute to write for half an hour in response to two sets of questions:

1) What did you like most about the institute? What is right just as it is and should never be changed?

2) What do you think can and should be improved and refined? What do you think we should do?

The codirector and I would leave the room during this time, always a little nervous, eager to get at those papers. After the good-byes, we closed the door, rushed to the papers—a quick look at first—and then we settled down to read them with great care. These responses remained as positive as they had been when we used the earlier forms, with numerous variations of "This was the best course I've ever taken!" However, instead of an off-the-chart score of 7+++, we also read comments on most everything that we had done or the teachers had done during the five weeks. The teachers didn't hold back in expressing their reactions to various parts of the institute or in suggesting ways in which the institute could be improved. For instance, over the years—with some notable exceptions—there was little interest in outside speakers: "You like *him*?" "Did you notice that she never once opened her eyes when she talked to us?" "He tries to come on as a down-home country sage." Guests were outsiders and not part of their project.

On their evaluations, teachers told us there were too many major writing assignments, not enough time to write, or not enough time to do everything we wanted them to do in the writing groups. These suggestions led to refinements: four papers instead of five, more alternative writing possibilities, and three afternoons a week in the writing groups instead of two. There were frequent complaints about being asked to read research articles that were written not for teachers but for other researchers and, as such, were frequently unreadable by those untrained in the jargon of academic research. So we gave more attention to collecting articles from which classroom practitioners would benefit. There were always urgings to find more free time for general discussion, which we did.

One year, because the answers to the first question—What did you like?—were mostly all positive and vague, I decided to drop that question and ask the summer fellows to comment only on how we could improve the institute. When we returned to the room to collect the forms, we faced a frustrated bunch who complained that they felt deprived. They wanted to write about how wonderful the summer had been, how perfect the institute and everything in it had been—the demonstrations by these great teachers, the supportive writing groups, the writing they had done, their pride at being able to call themselves writers and mean it, the friends they had made who they knew would be friends for life. Question one of the evaluation, I realized, was for the fellows, not for us, though I would be lying if I did not admit we enjoyed reading the rave reviews the institute received in response to that question. At any rate, I didn't make that mistake again.

∽ The Open Program: Casting a Wider Net ∽

Each summer, as BAWP continued, we invited twenty-five exemplary teachers of writing into the summer institute, but in the nine Bay Area counties, there are 176 school districts and hundreds of teachers with a keen interest in the teaching of writing. Clearly, we were missing a lot of talent. Traditionally, we relied heavily on the recommendations of past summer fellows to recruit new fellows. This method of recruitment had the effect of sending us candidates endorsed by someone who knew the program. But it also created an insularity.

In an effort to cast a wider net, we designed the BAWP open program, so named because it is open to any teacher who wants to attend. From the beginning, new teachers—even student teachers—and experienced teachers came to the program because they wanted to know more about teaching writing. The open program is designed much like the invitational program. It is coordinated by a staff of seasoned BAWP teacher-consultants. The self-selected participants usually meet for the first half of each morning in a large group to participate in a workshop conducted by a BAWP teacher-consultant, then they join smaller groups, each led by a staff member. In these smaller groups, teachers discuss the ideas and practices that surface during the presentations.

As is the case with teachers in the writing institute, editing/response groups also meet in the open program. At about the halfway point in the open program, the coordinators begin to invite selected teachers from the groups they are working with to demonstrate successful strategies from their own classrooms. Over the years, the open program has become a dependable source for future summer institute participants.

∽ School-Year Inservice ∽ Programs: Teachers Teaching Teachers

If National Writing Project programs were to begin and end with the summer institute, we would not be fulfilling our mission of improving writing and learning in the nation's schools. Twenty-five talented teachers sharing their best practices might have the effect of making these already skilled teachers even more expert, but it would do little to reform literacy education in America.

That's why school-year inservice programs were, and are, key to our work. To most teachers, "inservice" means a program conducted by an outside professional consultant who may not have been near a classroom in many years and who knows little about the circumstances of the teachers he or she is working with. Or, inservice may mean a publisher's representative pitching a particular program that a school district has adopted, with or without teacher input.

From the outset, the writing project adopted a different take on inservice. We believed that if school reform was to be effective, inservice programs must be conducted by the folks on the ground. Classroom teachers are the linchpin of reform. School reform can't happen just by passing laws, publishing mandates, requiring courses, or reading one more book. But real school reform can happen when teachers come together regularly throughout their careers to explore practices that effective teachers have already proven are successful in their classrooms. Inservice of this sort equals professional development, two terms that, alas, have not always been synonymous.

In the early days of the writing project, we developed some abiding principles and practices for presenting inservice.

- BAWP has always charged districts for inservice. In the beginning, it was a thousand dollars for ten three-hour programs. We have used the money to pay our teacher-consultants for their workshops and to administer the program. Our services have been a bargain compared with the prices charged by much more expensive, but sometimes less effective, consultants.

- When a district cannot afford a ten-session program, we have sometimes offered a five-workshop program, but with rare exceptions, we have refused to do a single-session program, which in fact has been the misguided norm for other purveyors of inservice. If teachers are to change as a result of these staff development programs, they need time to try out in their classrooms what the workshop is offering. They need to be able to report back on their successes and failures. This cannot happen when an expert drops in for one afternoon and then goes on his or her way.

- We have always insisted that our inservice programs be voluntary. We have not wanted to work with teachers who felt they were being held captive for three hours after school. By working with teachers keen on learning what we wanted to demonstrate, we are assured of enthusiastic participation. When other teachers, burned by condescending and ineffective inservice, have heard about this enthusiasm, they often want to join us.

- The success of an inservice series depends on having a talented coordinator. The coordinator's role is to talk with the school personnel to determine the specific needs of the group of teachers who will be involved, to help recruit the teacher–consultants who will make the presentations, to keep the records, and to provide links between the presentations.

- BAWP sessions have always been participatory. Our teacher–consultants do not give three-hour lectures. Typically, the coordinator will introduce the teacher–consultant, who then demonstrates a practice he or she has found valuable in teaching writing (frequently with sample student papers). And, after some discussion, the teachers are asked to do the writing inspired by this particular practice, to read aloud what they have composed, and to discuss the practice in more detail. The teachers are then encouraged to try out the practice in their classrooms, in cases where it is relevant, and to report at a later session on how it worked.

In many schools where we have worked, we have been invited back year after year. This seems to be clear evidence that we are doing something right.

THE PROJECT TO THE RESCUE

Over and over we hear the story of how the writing project has grabbed a teacher at just the right moment. Such was the case with high school science teacher and football coach Bob Tierney, who, as a teacher-consultant, would go on to conduct more workshops than any TC in the history of the writing project.

Here's how Bob described his early years in teaching: "My administrators were saying I was a good teacher, but I knew that what I was teaching could not be called science. My students were not thinking. They were just memorizing."

Bob seemed to reserve his real teaching for the weekend, when he assembled the Irvington High Seaweed Crew, a group of students who accompanied him and his family to Northern California's Tomales Bay on Friday nights, where they eventually identified 385 species of seaweed.

Mary Ann Smith picks up the story of Bob's transformation.

After twenty years, two books, and a Westinghouse fellowship to MIT, Bob "wanted out." He was dismayed by his visit to another teacher's fifth-grade class. "What I found was a teacher who was not spouting off information, whose class was actively involved. My class was too passive. This teacher had earned the right to be called 'teacher.' I could be replaced by a computer. The only things I did that made sense were the Seaweed Crew and the football team."

The call in 1980 from colleague Keith Caldwell came just in time. "I forgot to tell you," Keith said. "I nominated you for the Bay Area Writing Project Summer Institute." Bob momentarily tucked away his discouragement with teaching. He described in his institute interview the satisfactions of teaching biology to students who didn't want to learn it and his approaches to writing-to-learn. Most important were his experiments with audience: having students explain their learning to the people pictured in posters around his room.

He was accepted into the institute. "I remember our first meeting in the Faculty Club with real silverware. It was the first time as a teacher that I was treated as a professional and not condescended to." After the third day of the institute itself, Bob characterized his colleagues to his wife, Jackie, as "the most aggressive, intelligent group I've ever been with. I don't know if I'll last the summer."

First impressions. Bob had dozens of them. "What clicked right away was that writing itself—the process of writing—was the same as the scientific method. Hypothesize, experiment, revise your thinking—writing is a discovery process. Writing, in fact, is the vehicle for the scientific method."

To take his impressions beyond the institute and into his district's science classrooms was the next challenge. "The guys were already suspicious of me," Bob remembers. "I'd been trying out some new technique, and as my good friend Harry said, 'Tierney, you spent five weeks with a bunch of poets.'" Bob proposed that together the science teachers test the theory that more writing in science classes would help students understand science better. "When it doesn't work, we'll march back to Berkeley and let them know about it," Bob promised. One by one, his colleagues backed away. "I have a whole garage of Amway to sell," a friend explained. But Harry said okay.

The experiment centered on a genetics unit. "Harry taught it the way we had for twenty-five years, lots of memorization, answers to end-of-the-chapter questions, that sort of thing," Bob explains. "I used writing project writing-to-learn ideas. We gave pre- and post-tests. Harry's kids did slightly better on the post-test. It was very disappointing." Sixteen weeks later, however, both teachers gave the unit test again. Bob's students recalled 19 percent more than Harry's.

"At the end of the term, we changed techniques. Harry used writing and I used the old way. This time, Harry's kids [the writers] did better. We couldn't draw a scientific conclusion, but we had evidence about writing and retention. The most important thing," Bob emphasizes, "was that the science department was having meetings at the local pizza parlor and talking about the ways kids learn instead of gossiping or making excuses like we'd done in the past. Eventually, other science teachers at other schools began to come to the pizza parlor, and then the district gave us a site and started releasing us. We ended up with thirty-five teachers brainstorming about what we could do to help kids learn science. We came from the ground floor, which is the strength of the writing project."

Rejuvenated, Bob was no longer looking for a new job, but the writing project did give him some new and important work. He became one of our major presenters on the subject of writing-to-learn. He has given workshops in twenty-five states, and in one year talked with six thousand teachers from coast to coast. Working with science and other teachers outside of English departments, he may have done more than any other educator to defuse the phrase still too often heard in teachers' lounges: "Writing? That's what they're supposed to teach in English class."

⤜ Continuity Programs: ⤛
How a Writing Project Becomes a Community

Follow-through has always been a key to the success of our inservice programs, but what about follow-through programs for the teacher-consultants (TCs) themselves? As should be clear by now, the summer institute has often been a professional and emotional high for our summer fellows. But, as the laws of physics proclaim, what goes up must come down. The question we faced early on was, How do we help our TCs maintain their institute-fed energy, enthusiasm, and sense of community once they have reentered the bureaucratic and negative atmosphere persistent in too many schools?

Our answer has been to provide year-round activities—continuity programs—that TCs will find compelling. At BAWP, continuity programs start with our monthly Saturday meetings. Most of these sessions take the form of workshops presented by experienced BAWP teacher-consultants as well as fellows from the most recent institute. These sessions give new TCs a chance to sharpen their skills before they take the plunge into inservice school programs. Experienced TCs often use the Saturday morning platform to make public new strategies that have been successful in their classrooms, but which they have kept under wraps. While these meetings are open to any teacher, administrator, or parent who wants to attend—and many from all these constituencies do come—the primary function of these sessions is to bring the clan of teacher-consultants together to socialize, compare professional notes, and once again learn from one another.

Over the years, BAWP, particularly under the leadership of Carol Tateishi, its current director, has added a potpourri of continuity programs all intended to keep our teacher-consultants involved with our work. BAWP has a spring writing retreat, a teacher research group, and a working group that focuses on improving our inservice. A group of BAWP teachers has traveled to El Salvador, visiting schools and working with teaching colleagues there. BAWP holds regular readings for its teacher-authors at local bookstores, and each summer dozens of BAWP teacher-consultants work in BAWP programs, such as the open institute and the Young Writers Program.

Significantly, many of these ideas did not originate with BAWP. Rather, we picked up on these notions by keeping our eyes and ears open to what was happening at other sites in the National Writing Project network. In the writing project, no site has a monopoly on good ideas. Recognizing this, sites learn from one another, just as writing project teachers learn from one another.

THE DEVELOPMENT OF THE CALIFORNIA AND NATIONAL WRITING PROJECTS

⮑ *Writing Becomes Respectable* ⮐

BY 1976, THE BAY AREA WRITING PROJECT had evolved into more than just a good idea percolating as we sat on the deck of Sam's Cafe in Tiburon, California. We now had two years of successful experience conducting our invitational summer institute and our teachers-teaching-teachers school-year inservice program.

Because we had actually done something, we thought we should again apply for funding. We decided to go back to the National Endowment for the Humanities (NEH) with another proposal. The NEH had by now changed its policy to include writing as one of the fundable humanities. This time we paid careful attention to the pointed advice Alden Dunham had given us at the time of our original proposal. "I look first at the budget and evaluation sections," he had said. Believing that the program officer at the Carnegie Foundation would know what he was talking about, we gave special attention to these sections. I contacted Michael Scriven, whom Dunham had previously recommended to do our evaluation. He agreed to take on this responsibility. As for the budget, I knew I needed to take Dunham's advice and get somebody other than me to do the job. But when I began to interview "budget people," I realized that they had no understanding of what we were doing. We could barely talk to each other. They knew nothing about the world of education, writing, or the writing project. Then it dawned on me. I had my budget person right under my nose: Miles Myers. Miles was already working for the writing project while on leave from the Oakland schools, and in addition to his responsibilities as an educator, he kept the books for his wife's three day-care centers and just generally knew about numbers. In addition, he had years of administrative and political experience as ongoing vice president of the California Federation of Teachers. Miles agreed to the job. When we submitted our application, the budget and evaluation sections had some meat on their bones. This time NEH funded us.

But that wasn't all. About a week after we received this good news, Bill Russell, our program officer at NEH, called.

"Would you be interested in writing an amendment to your proposal?" he said. "We think you should request additional funds to help other universities establish their own Bay Area Writing Projects." The writing project, he said, was too good a program to be located at UC Berkeley alone. Later, immersed in the struggle for money that was to plague the writing project for many years, I would think back fondly on those words: "We think you should request additional funds . . ."

Flattering and enticing as this invitation was, I had to tell Bill that I'd get back to him. I called Rod Park, who had supported us all this time, and he set up a meeting in the chancellor's office with senior UC administrators who were interested in the project. I had the job of convincing them that Berkeley's interest in the project would not be compromised if we accepted NEH's invitation to expand our work. My argument was that we had already helped establish new writing projects at Duke University and at Oregon State University, Ashland. The directors of those new sites were committed to following the BAWP model, but they were responsible for running their own projects and free to make the BAWP model work in their own geographic areas. The Bay Area Writing Project would continue to do what it set out to do: improve the teaching of writing in Bay Area schools. It wasn't a hard sell. If UC Berkeley could be identified with improving the teaching of writing in the nation's schools, why would these university administrators complain?

The NEH wished to make a public statement about this new project that accented university-school collaboration. This was a new tack for the endowment, which viewed creating a network of Bay Area Writing Projects as having extraordinary promise of national scope. The program directors at NEH wanted to announce their new program in California, and together we planned a press conference that brought Ronald Berman, chairman of the NEH, and Wilson Riles, superintendent of schools for California, to Las Lomas High School in Walnut

Creek to speak to the nation's press.

Simultaneously with the NEH proposal, we had submitted another proposal to the Carnegie Corporation of New York. Alden Dunham, the program officer from Carnegie, visited the project occasionally on his frequent trips to San Francisco to make sure we were writing a proposal he wanted to read. He already had a strong feel for the project, and he knew what he wanted to fund. "We know the project works; now we want to find out why it works." The Carnegie grant funded a three-year evaluation of the Bay Area Writing Project, and it named Michael Scriven as the evaluator.

Scriven was an expert in evaluation, he did his work mostly as a UC Berkeley professor of philosophy. He had a dominating presence, always dressing as if he were about to make a trek across the veldt with his khaki shirt and trousers and holstered knife. I was delighted that he and his graduate students were interested in taking on this project.

⌒ Judging BAWP: It's No Passing Fad ⌒

MILES MYERS TOOK IT UPON HIMSELF to serve as liaison between Scriven's evaluation project and BAWP. It soon became evident that we had problems. Scriven's basic design—there were various studies over this three-year evaluation—focused on students in grades ten to twelve who were taught by teachers who had participated in BAWP invitational summer institutes. This was not what we had expected, and we believed Scriven had it backward. Why study the impact the project was having in the classrooms of some of the Bay Area's best writing teachers when we were bringing these teachers together to prepare them to teach *other teachers* how to teach writing more effectively? That was the heart of our staff development project and the focus of our teachers-teaching-teachers idea, and it was that idea we wanted Scriven to evaluate. Miles spent hours in difficult private meetings arguing this issue with Scriven.

In 1978, Scriven invited the Educational Testing Service's Paul B. Diederich, the dean of evaluators in the field of English and author of the important *Measuring Growth in English,* to the project as consultant. Scriven had immense regard for Paul

Diederich. He told us a number of stories about what Paul had accomplished. One such story has Paul solving a major problem when the Educational Testing Service brought a number of university faculty and classroom teachers together to score the first College Boards writing samples. The papers were handed out, and the scorers began to read and mark them up the same way they had always done when grading student papers. It didn't take long before everyone knew that this wasn't going to work. If they'd kept at it that way, the scorers would still be there. So, as the story goes, Paul Diederich launched holistic scoring, a one-to-five ranking of papers, based on certain criteria agreed upon among the scorers.

When Paul returned to Princeton, he put together a detailed report based on everything he had noted during his visit, which included interviews with BAWP's staff, Scriven and his staff, and classroom teachers and observations of evaluation sessions. Paul's report to me, which I passed on to Scriven, seemed to have an effect on Scriven's thinking. He wrote:

> *Now let me take a broader view of this whole problem of evaluating what BAWP has accomplished so far and is likely to accomplish in the near future. First, I believe you have something red-hot going for you. I could not estimate how many meetings, workshops, and cooperative projects of English teachers I have participated in over the past forty years, but I know that the usual attitude is one of polite skepticism interspersed with strong opposition. I seldom get the feeling that these teachers are going to do anything about the ideas expressed in these meetings. But here in the Bay Area you have a large group of intelligent and well-informed teachers whose attitudes toward BAWP methods of training and rejuvenating teachers are wildly enthusiastic. They are not only applying the ideas they have picked up in their own teaching but are also eager to spread the word with apostolic zeal. Even those who fear that the enthusiasm generated by this movement will not show up in the short papers written by students all hope that its beneficial effects will be proven by other means in the short run, and by improvement in writing in the long run.*

Here in New Jersey we have a writing improvement program reaching thousands of students, directed by Professor Janet Emig of Rutgers University, who is an extremely competent teacher and researcher. I think her program will do a great deal of good, but it is not of the sort that attracts nationwide attention. One never hears teachers in Florida to Texas talking about it or coming to New Jersey to find out what is going on. But I have been getting bits and pieces of information about the Bay Area project ever since it started, even though no article has been published about it that gave the whole picture of what it is about. The basic ideas of the project that reached me by word of mouth seemed so practical and attractive that I have long wanted to get a close look at it to find out whether it really works as well as the rumors say. My visit to the reading session last month convinced me that, whether or not it has yet reached a stage at which it can demonstrate effects on student writing, it has stirred up English teachers to an extent that I have seldom if ever seen. I was closely involved in the work of some of the research and development centers established by Project English, but none of them started what one would call a "movement." I now believe that the Bay Area Writing Project really has started a movement that is sweeping the country.

Thus it is well on its way toward passing the "test of the market," and we have only to wait a few years to find out whether it is a passing fad or a basic idea that will leave a mark on the training of English teachers long after the initial excitement has subsided. With all my bias in favor of hard data, I am already pretty sure that this is one of those ideas that will last—like Langdell's invention of the case method of teaching law about 1870.

In the summary of his own evaluation, Scriven didn't say much about the effect of our work on the teachers in the inservice programs, as we wished he would, but his general conclusion was a great support to our efforts. "[The writing project] appears to be the best large-scale effort to improve composition instruction now in operation in this country, and certainly is the best on which substantial data are available." Scriven told me that he wished he could have done better for us. He acknowledged he was getting anecdotal evidence by the bushel from 1974 summer fellows, who were saying that their students were improving because of the impact the project had on their teaching. I still would have liked to have seen an evaluation that was closer to the design we were pushing for. I knew that many of the teachers who had participated in BAWP's school-year programs had become excellent teachers of writing and had surfaced as future summer fellows because of it, but there was no way accurate data could be collected from such a diverse group of teachers teaching in such diverse situations—both Diederich and Scriven were positive about that. Scriven did have an influence on me. His focus on what the summer fellows were learning from one another and what impact they were having on their own students made me realize as never before that these excellent teachers we were bringing together to teach other teachers were just as eager to learn more about writing and the teaching of writing as were the teachers they taught in our school-year inservice programs.

The Beginnings of a Statewide Network

WHEN BILL WEBSTER, California's enthusiastic deputy superintendent of instruction, heard of the NEH's grant and their interest in supporting staff development programs, he called me to propose meetings in three widely separate areas—Los Angeles, San Jose, and Chico. He wanted to make sure that faculty from all of the campuses of the University of California and California State University heard about the NEH offer to support additional Bay Area Writing Projects at universities throughout the state. It was a great idea.

The agendas would be the same at all three meetings. Bill Webster would act as chair, and a classroom teacher from BAWP and I would talk about the project.

In Southern California, we met at the Kellogg Conference Center, high atop a hill overlooking the California State University, Pomona campus. I took away one sharp memory from this meeting. Ev Jones, the distinguished chairman of the UCLA Subject A department, told us that he knew very well what it was about the Bay Area Writing Project that made it so successful with classroom teachers: "It is a program that is one-third curriculum, one-third group therapy, and one-third religious experience." While Ev said this tongue in cheek, his was the first comment of many to follow that tried to pin down why the Bay Area Writing Project had such a strong hold on teachers.

At all three sessions, the questions and the comments from the floor made it apparent that we had raised some keen interest. I informed the audience that fifteen-thousand-dollar grants were now available from BAWP to help new projects get started. These grants would be awarded based on competitive review. Matching grants of an additional fifteen thousand dollars would be required. The NEH insisted upon this matching fund provision, and it has become a continuing and wise policy throughout the history of the writing project. The federal funds we now receive are described in law as matching funds. Each year established sites as well as potential sites must provide a match for their continuing and new grants. This policy has encouraged additional funding from host universities and local schools and districts in the project's service area, but it also has helped sites tap a wide range of additional funding sources: state and local foundations, businesses and industries in their immediate areas, individual donors, and any other sources an imaginative director can think of.

~

When we had received all of the new site applications from California universities and from a few others beyond California's boundaries, Miles and I took them to my house one night. We spread them out on the front room carpet and began reading. At the end of the evening, we selected eight of the eleven applications submitted by California universities and three submitted by universities in other states. (We had an agreement with Bill Russell to limit the number of new projects in California so that we could support projects in different areas of the country.) These were the sites we chose:

1. University of California, Los Angeles/Santa Monica College
2. University of California, Santa Cruz

3. University of California, Davis/California State University, Sacramento
4. University of California, San Diego
5. University of California, Riverside/California State University, San Bernardino
6. California State University, Sonoma
7. California State Universities at Dominguez Hills, Fullerton, and Long Beach/University of Southern California
8. California State University, Chico
9. Rutgers University, New Jersey
10. University of Colorado, Boulder
11. Pace College/BOCES, New York

At this time, I was still thinking that our relationship with these projects would be the same as the one we had with Duke University and Oregon State University, Ashland. That is, we would help universities across the country establish their own, independently run Bay Area Writing Projects. The site in upstate New York even named itself the Bay Area Writing Project East. The only difference would be that we now had gift and matching funds to help universities get started. When we finished our review, I had no thought of establishing networks, no thought of establishing a statewide California Writing Project, no thought of establishing a National Writing Project.

It didn't take long, however—only a day or two—to realize the dimensions of what we were doing. With funds from NEH, we had established a nine-site statewide California writing project—BAWP plus the eight new writing projects—and, by counting the projects we had already helped in North Carolina and Oregon plus the three new projects we were now helping in Colorado, New York, and New Jersey, we had also established, more by accident than by design, a fourteen-site national network—the National Writing Project.

While the National Writing Project network has grown enormously since its beginnings in 1976–77, the idea that created that network has remained constant: we decided then that the National Writing Project would be a federation of independent and locally administered writing project sites based on the Bay Area

Writing Project model and program design and held together by common philosophy, goals, and basic assumptions and by the glue of networking provided initially by the Bay Area Writing Project and later by the greatly expanded networking programs of the National Writing Project.

THE MISSISSIPPI STORY,
OR HOW FEDERAL FUNDING CAME
TO THE NATIONAL WRITING PROJECT

Just as BAWP has a unique story to tell, so do most National Writing Project sites. Of these, no story is more compelling than that of the writing project sites in Mississippi, which almost single-handedly put in motion the dynamic that generated congressional funding for our work.

Yet the Mississippi story shares ingredients with the narratives of other sites: a strong leader committed to improving the teaching of writing in her home territory, a talented cadre of teachers ready to go to work, and a receptive community that understands the importance of writing as a life skill.

Here Mary Ann Smith tells the story of Sandra Burkett, who provided the vision and the leg work that made possible the Mississippi network of writing projects and, beyond that, was the catalyst for national funding of the National Writing Project.

The National Writing Project was eleven years old before Mississippi joined us. But ever since then, the state has been making up for lost time. It was, after all, the Mississippi project that inspired a United States senator to sponsor legislation to support the entire NWP with national funding.

In Mississippi, I have been told, talking on a front porch, following a dream, listening for the spirit to move you—these are more typical ways of getting to the heart of things. And so, on a beach in Biloxi in August 1983, Mississippi State professor Sandra Burkett noted in her journal that she wanted to become a writer, and what's more, she wanted to do something about writing in Mississippi schools.

Sandra knew that the second of these ambitions would cost money. And for all she protests as she recounts the story—"I was just a Mississippi girl who had never been anywhere except to an occasional conference"—Sandra had the savvy of a professional fund-raiser. "I went to Washington, made appointments with several federal agencies, and asked people to give me money to do something about writing in Mississippi. When I went to The Fund for the Improvement of Postsecondary Education, the people there told me about the National Writing Project. The National Institute of Education loaded me up with books and research and gave me Jim Gray's phone number. Then I went to the National Endowment for the Humanities, and they also gave me Jim's telephone number. 'He'll be glad to talk to you,' they said." Sandra takes a breath before her next confession. "I had heard of BAWP. A colleague across campus had sent around a blurb from a journal about teachers teaching teachers. I had dismissed it as the blind leading the blind."

But she soon had a change of heart. By December 1983, Sandra had a planning grant and an invitation from Jim Gray to visit Berkeley the following summer, where she settled on the Bay Area Writing Project model, in spite of her previous reservations. "I visited the BAWP institute a couple of mornings, and I knew that this was what Mississippi needed. I remember a quiet English teacher demonstrating her approach through her students' work, and another teacher who taught English and sang like Pavarotti."

In the summer of 1985, nineteen teachers joined Sandra Burkett for the first summer institute at Mississippi State in Starkville. "Our program would have been dead in the water without a site visit from the National Writing Project. That set the tone for the success of our whole project. All of us still remember the workshop on writing as a process, a concept that was new to us at the time. And all of us remember the teacher who dramatically confessed in her first piece of writing that she was a writing teacher who never wrote. She discovered herself that summer."

The institute took on a life of its own. "People who lived in the dorm stayed up all night, reading and responding to each other and tasting from a whole array of books."

Afterward, Sandra and her writing project embarked on a new life. "The fellows went back and sold the idea of inservice to their districts, and the districts contracted with us," Sandra remembers. "Two of the teacher-consultants were released together for twenty-five days to go out and work for the project. At this point, my attitude was, 'Call me if you need me.' The key to the whole thing is trusting the teachers. I came to believe that the teachers could do a better job than I could, so I set them loose to do it."

Almost immediately, the project started branching out. "I went everywhere they'd let me," says Sandra, "and talked about the project." The schools in the state capital, Jackson, were in a hurry to have their own project. Sandra set up an invitational institute and began with a one-week session, followed by a series of released days, with urban teachers relying on substitutes to teach their classes. "This was not a good way to do it. The teachers kept worrying about their kids, so it was hard to keep the focus," she admits. In spite of the drawbacks, the combination of Starkville and Jackson teacher-consultants conducted seven inservice series for Jackson teachers the following year.

Nor were teachers in other parts of the state to be denied. In 1986, they found new sites waiting for them at Southern Mississippi University and Delta State University, and in 1987 at the University of Mississippi, "Ole Miss." The idea of a network of Mississippi writing project sites began to emerge. "Here's where the behind-the-scenes work was most important," Sandra explains, "meeting with school superintendents, teachers, PTA members, school administrators, foundation people, anyone who wanted to support us. We worked hard to be sensitive to the politics of our state, waiting to declare ourselves a network until the jewel—Ole Miss—had joined us." Since 1987, three historically Black universities have also become part of the network: Jackson State, Mississippi Valley State, and Alcorn State.

But to understand how this network changed the entire National Writing Project, one must understand the nature of relationships in Mississippi. Everything seems to begin with friendships, with seeking out once-upon-a-time acquaintances, with knowing someone who knows someone else.

Sherry Swain, a first-grade teacher in Starkville and a summer fellow in the first institute at Mississippi State University (and now director of the MSU Writing/Thinking Project), came to Sandra one day and said in her quiet way, "My daddy has a friend in the capital. They think what we're doing deserves state funding, and they want to do something. I don't know whether to say yes or no."

"Well, don't say no," Sandra said.

Sandra and Sherry went down to the state capital and met with the Senate Education Subcommittee. They showed their videotape, and Sherry did most of the talking. "This was a teacher telling her story," Sandra recalls.

Then Sherry had another announcement. "Thad Cochran [the U.S. senator from Mississippi] is going to be out at the airport, and Daddy wants a packet of materials to take to him. Oh yes, Sandra, and Daddy says your former student is Senator Cochran's education aide."

In Mississippi, friends watch over friends. With the help of Sandra's former student, Anne Cherry, Senator Cochran became increasingly interested in the National Writing Project. By the time Sandra, Jim Gray, and Don Gallehr, director of the Northern Virginia Writing Project, met with the senator, he was a receptive audience. In fact, Sandra says, "He told us the story of being the son of two teachers. He remembered his mother and daddy going out and doing staff development for other teachers, so he understood our model, and he made a commitment to helping us get this money."

Thus, the state that found its way into the National Writing Project later than most others brought with it federal funding for all sites. "That our senator sponsored that legislation has kept our state funding alive," Sandra says. "And we're so pleased to give something back to this project that gave us the model that has worked so well in our state. This is Mississippi's gift to the project."

NETWORKS WITHIN THE NETWORK

One strength of the National Writing Project is that it is national. We have a model that has affected positively the quality of staff development in most every state. But, if we aren't careful, one limitation of our project may be that it is national. Our model needs to give attention to regional and other differences or we will be no better than the top-down structures we seek to replace. One way we have dealt with this national complexity is to create regional and special-interest networks that work toward shared solutions. Here Ann Dobie, director of the National Writing Project of Acadiana and the first director of the Rural Sites Network, writes of that network's first meeting.

Joye Alberts, my codirector, and I held our breath when we pulled chairs into a circle at the first meeting of the fledgling Rural Sites Network in Louisville, Kentucky, in 1992. We made a small one, just in case nobody came, but to our relief and wonder we had to keep adding chairs to accommodate our fellow rural site directors. Our single question for the breakout session was: "Is there a need for a Rural Sites Network in the National Writing Project?" The answer that came from the expanding circle was a resounding yes. Clearly, these directors considered themselves the "Other," the "silent," the marginalized. It turned out that "the unheard" had plenty to say. They talked of serving large areas that make it hard to attract teachers to summer institutes, maintain continuity programs, and provide inservice workshops. They agreed that cultural differences sometimes make rural school authorities suspicious of university personnel and reluctant to change, and they recognized that they serve multicultural populations, including the poor, who live in situations different from those found in inner cities. We realized, with surprise bordering on shock, that we were talking about problems and strengths we had thought were ours alone. When someone from South Dakota commented that the principals in her area weren't too sure they wanted teachers from "the outside" to import new ideas into their schools, her counterpart from Pennsylvania found it easy to say, "I know, I know."

I realized then that the only surprising aspect of the Rural Sites Network was that it hadn't sprung up earlier. It was inevitable.

~

For better or worse, creative financing was very much a part of early writing project history. We needed money to jump-start our programs, and Miles Myers had a gift for finding it. Because Miles had always maintained his tie to the Oakland schools, he delighted in coming up with ideas that would benefit Oakland as well as the writing project. One of these ideas was to tap into Title IVC funds. Title IVC was a federal program administered by the states to stimulate innovative practices in the schools. The California Title IVC program granted money to school districts to implement projects that, if deemed "exemplary" under scrutiny by the state, would be funded on an ongoing basis.

The year after we received our initial grants from Carnegie and NEH, Miles wrote a Title IVC grant proposal for the Oakland Unified School District to support staff development. When Miles received news that his proposal was funded in the amount of ten thousand dollars, he had the idea that other writing project sites throughout California might, with a few changes, find his Oakland proposal a usable model. So he mailed his proposal to all California Writing Project (CWP) sites with a cover letter that explained his plan:

- The Oakland Title IVC development grant proposal could be the basis for other district proposals simply by replacing every reference to Oakland with the names of participating districts in each site's service area.
- If funded, each district would contribute the ten thousand dollars in grant money to the grant pool administered by the local CWP site.
- All participating districts would share the pool money equally, whether funded or not.

The local districts liked the idea and agreed to support the plan. Most applied and several were funded. By this point, the state was recognizing the writing project as an exemplary program and not asking too many questions. Eugene Soules, director of the North Bay Writing Project, didn't even bother erasing the name Oakland from the text of Miles's proposal. He simply put a new title on the original grant proposal and added his name and local address. His proposal was approved for funding nevertheless.

The next part of Miles's plan was to make it possible for local sites to receive Title IVC funds directly and continually. Although Jack Schuster, the director of IVC in California, was initially supportive—he and Miles had in fact set up the Title IVC plan together—he was now worried about being swamped by CWP proposals to the detriment of other district proposals, and he turned down this stage of our plan. Not to be stopped, Miles and I drove to Sacramento and put the plan before Wilson Riles, the state superintendent of public instruction. Riles was open to the idea of having the California Writing Project supported by Title IVC. The record of California's Title IVC grants was uneven. The state had bet on some pretty flimsy programs. Why not, reasoned Miles, support a program with a proven track record. At the close of our meeting, he approved Miles's plan. The Bay Area Writing Project was named "exemplary" by California's Title IVC. This status was renewed year after year, and over the next six years Title IVC provided the California Writing Project with eight hundred thousand dollars in additional support. (In 1977–78, the Oregon writing project received an eighty-five-thousand-dollar Title IVC Development Grant with a proposal based on the BAWP model, and the Oklahoma project and all of the Virginia writing projects also received Title IVC grants.)

I did not go into education because I was fond of writing grant proposals, and as Miles demonstrated, there are people far more skilled in this area than I am. But, that said, it should be noted that the writing project has survived and thrived because we have been able to explain our work to those who manage the purse strings.

ᨒ California Discovers BAWP ᨒ

ROD PARK, provost and dean of the College of Letters and Science at UC Berkeley, continued to support financially the Bay Area Writing Project, but as the years went by, he realized this line item in his university budget could not be maintained. It needed to be picked up by the California State Legislature. The Bay Area Writing Project and its offshoot, the California Writing Project, were expanding and needed new levels of support for a range of expenses: for released stipends for summer fellows and teacher-consultants and inservice coordinators, money for a growing publications program, travel expenses to state and national sites and to CWP and NWP annual meetings, and fund-raising expenses.

In 1978, Park began talking to his friend Donald Swain who, as vice president of the University of California, annually presented the regents' budget to the legislature. Swain had always been keenly interested in the writing project. Years later, when he left the UC Office of the President to become president of the University of Louisville, one of his first moves was to secure a writing project site on the Louisville campus. Year after year, as long as he was university president, he provided the Kentucky Writing Project at Louisville with secure funding.

Swain began discussing this idea of legislative support for the California Writing Project with his counterpart within the California State University (CSU) system. A number of CWP sites were on CSU campuses, and Swain wanted—and needed—strong agreement from CSU before he could move forward. CSU was delighted with what UC was planning and agreed to support the continuing administration of the California Writing Project on the UC Berkeley campus.

In 1978–79, with all of the plans worked out, Swain invited me to join his committee to testify before the Senate Finance Committee. This was a new and exciting adventure for me. When the day arrived, I felt well prepared. However, things didn't go as I had imagined. The hearings took place in a large committee room with stadium seating. Those testifying sat low in a pit and looked up at the senators, who sat behind a long judicial bench high above us, reminiscent of the bench in the U.S. Supreme Court. Vice President Swain went first, and when he was finished speaking, he had me take his seat in the pit. I had hardly begun my remarks about the writing project and its teachers–teaching–teachers model and my purpose in testifying, when the committee chairman, a bull-like man with a huge bald head, looked down at me and sharply asked, "Why didn't you train them right the first time?" I was given no time to respond, as the chairman began talking to other members of the committee. I do remember being asked a question by Senator Petrie, but I have no memory of what the question was.

However, at that moment I began to understand that if we were going to work with government, we would need to learn to better explain ourselves in the political arena. Despite this less-than-auspicious start, the following year, the California Analyst's Office of the California Legislature supported the University of California's request for a three-hundred-thousand-dollar general fund augmentation to provide a permanent base of support for the California Writing Project. The California Legislature agreed, and the funds were put into the general fund in the regents' budget.

ᕮ *More Service, More Work* ᕮ

AS OUR FUNDING INCREASED, so did our workload. We often came to work before eight in the morning and stayed late into the evening. Yet our energy level remained high. We were building a larger staff, and we were feeling like a team. Miles Myers became administrative director, and for four years his administrative assistant was Cathy Hill, a former high school student of his, followed by Mary Schoenfeldt for six more years. Mary K. Healy replaced Cap Lavin as codirector, and Keith Caldwell joined the staff after he convinced the Fremont Unified School District that they would get more out of him if he worked for the writing project than if he continued his curriculum work at Fremont. The district released him to work with the project with full salary and benefits, and it continued this arrangement for the next three years. Keith established and edited the popular *NWP Network Newsletter*. He took on projects that interested him, and with his wry, disarming humor, he became a natural troubleshooter for the project. Ken Lane edited an early BAWP publication, *The California High School Proficiency Examination: Evaluating the Writing Samples* by Ruby Bernstein and Barney Tanner, participants in the first BAWP summer institute. This became volume one, number one in the new *Curriculum, Evaluation, and Research* series publication program that Gerry Camp, who was already director of the open program during the summers, continued and expanded when he became BAWP's editor. Gerry soon had twenty additional studies underway as well as a number of "Occasional Papers." *Teaching Writing K-12* by Jack Hailey was published in collaboration with the UC Berkeley School of Education, and a few years later, NCTE published an anthology drawn from these BAWP publications, as did Heinemann Publishers. This expanded publication program soon had teachers becoming researchers. They wrote descriptions of their teaching and their classrooms. Along with our various staff development programs, our publishing program became another powerful way to disseminate information and practices gathered through the writing project.

The number of coordinators for our school-year inservice programs increased as the number of school contracts increased, and because coordinators participated in every workshop of every BAWP inservice series, they began to have greater power in shaping each series, including inviting the teacher-consultants they thought would work best for each program. During Mary K. Healy's tenure as BAWP codirector in charge of inservice programs, the number of year-long school-year programs eventually increased to more than eighty, and the cost to districts for a full ten-session series increased over time from one thousand dollars to over three thousand dollars.

With so much happening, the Bay Area Writing Project received increased national attention in the press. Articles appeared in the *New York Times* and the *Los Angeles Times,* and an Associated Press story was reprinted nationwide. *American Education* and *Phi Delta Kappan* published articles about the Bay Area Writing Project. BAWP was featured in ABC and CBS documentaries on American education, and I was invited to appear on PBS's *McNeil/Lehrer Report.*

As a result of all this attention, we were being contacted regularly by colleges and universities throughout the country who wanted to start writing project sites. NEH liked this; from early on they saw the Bay Area Writing Project as a national model. We, of course, were eager to proselytize the teachers-teaching-teachers idea. We did not have a formal review process of the sort that is in place today, but we did make sure that anyone who wanted to start a site was grounded in our principles.

At the end of 1978, the Bay Area Writing Project received the seventh annual Western Electric Fund Appreciation Award "in recognition of outstanding achievement in meeting today's educational needs."

⤝ *Organizing the National Writing Project* ⤞

THE FIRST NATIONAL MEETING for local National Writing Project (NWP) site directors was held in a dimly lit ballroom in an old hotel in Kansas City in 1978. I had never before seen all our directors together in one place. We put chairs in a circle so that the thirty or so in attendance could easily see one another and talk. As directors told their stories of successes and problems, for the first time it felt like we were part of a national organization.

Our directors meeting at the NCTE Convention became an annual event for us, as did, a few years later, our directors meeting during the NCTE Spring Conference. One of my fondest memories of working with the other NWP directors occurred at one of these NWP Spring Meetings. In the fall sometime during the late 1980s, I had become upset with a number of California site directors for straying from the basic writing project model. Adherence to the model had always been something of an obsession with me. While I know that different sites have different obstacles and different needs, I have always taken on the job of reminding the sites of the key elements of our success, such as the invitational summer institute and the teachers-teaching-teachers inservice program—those features that distinguish us from less successful school reform efforts. I wrote a letter to the CWP directors reminding them that all of our sites were based on the same model, and I spelled out, in categories, the components of that model in a list that ran about two to three pages. I thought it was good letter, a bit thin, but clear and to the point. When I began planning the agenda of the Spring Meeting, I thought of my letter to the CWP and had an idea: I would pass out copies of the letter to the directors, put them in small groups, and ask each director to read the list of components with some care and then suggest how each component could be improved, so that we could send a more detailed letter to all of the NWP sites. I asked them to give me what they had written by the end of the meeting and told them I would use what I could in putting together the improved letter. Their enthusiasm was palpable. They quickly went to work. When I read what they had written, I found something of value on every page, new ideas that had not occurred to me, phrasing superior to anything I would have thought of. It was an unparalleled team effort. Putting the results together, I had a thirteen-page NWP publication that I titled, "Basic Components of the NWP Staff Development Project Model and Program Design" (see appendix).

As the project grew from fourteen sites in the first year of outside funding (1976–77) to forty-one sites the second year and sixty-nine sites the third year, our structures became more sophisticated. We asked our network of sites to prepare annual reports because we needed current data and information to support our increasing grant campaign. As growth continued, we established regional blocks and appointed an NWP regional director for each area.

How the Writing Project Became Inclusive

The writing project is about teachers teaching teachers, and in recent decades these words have come to refer especially to what teachers of color have to teach the rest of us. Our goal has always been a writing project that is truly inclusive. And now, especially under the leadership of Richard Sterling, we are taking giant steps in that direction. But as Denise Patmon, codirector of the Boston Writing Project points out here, the road toward diversity has not been without its bumps.

It was November 1981. The ballroom seemed exceptionally large. The faces were White, predominantly male, and chiefly university types. I remember wondering, "How did I locate myself (Black and female) in this room?"

I came to the meeting of National Writing Project site directors as a representative of the Boston Writing Project (BWP), which has been multiracial and multicultural since its inception in 1979. Housed at the University of Massachusetts at Boston, a public university with an urban mission, BWP originated in the final moments of the dramatic struggle over court-ordered desegregation of the Boston public schools. Irate adults stoned yellow school buses, and the wide-eyed but tearful faces of brave children permeated the news about Boston during the mid-to-late 1970s. Prior to busing, some folks in the Northeast were quite apt to think that racism and discrimination were Southern problems, as though they existed only in the South. Boston, a cradle of liberty and of the abolitionist movement, became a symbol of the fact that racism, racial hatred, and discrimination thrived in New England as well.

The battle over desegregating the Boston public schools served as an anchor for change and inclusion among a variety of institutions in the area, which had heretofore been racially and ethnically exclusive.

Attending the 1981 site directors meeting, I was thoroughly immersed in and optimistic about our work with a diverse group of teachers on the local level. I was anxious and enthusiastic about meeting writing project teachers and directors on a national level. My first impression of NWP was admirable yet haunting. There was a lot of good energy in the room, much excitement, plenty of talk about writing everywhere; yet I was stunned to be what seemed like one Black person among hundreds of White persons. I recall saying to my BWP colleagues Peter Golden and Joe Check something like, "Hey, don't Black folks teach writing and lead writing projects? Are they meeting in another room as a caucus or something?" They acknowledged awareness of the "White out," too.

At the end of that November day in 1981, although I had found the meeting informative, invigorating, and even inspiring, I knew that if I was to have an ongoing relationship at the national level, something had to be done about the lack of racial and cultural diversity. There were boundaries that had to be pushed.

Talking about this specific goal with a few of my new writing project colleagues, like Richard Sterling, Sheridan Blau, and others, made me feel encouraged and assured that I was not alone in wanting to act on this obvious need. I remember the following day at the NCTE Black Caucus meeting, I stood up and made a special point to publicize NWP, to do what I later learned Jim Gray does—to cast a net, so others might investigate this marvelous network. The room remained silent after my announcement. Later, a caucus colleague turned to me and whispered, "Girl, what are you doing in that White People's Project?" Indeed, there was a lot of work to be done and boundaries to be expanded.

Since 1981, NWP has been at work on diversity and inclusion. One defining moment for me in this struggle came in the mid-1980s when BWP leadership was invited to Lehman College to work with New York City Writing Project (NYCWP) teacher-consultants around issues related to teaching writing in our respective city schools. At this meeting, Linette Moorman (now NYCWP director) provided an interesting analysis of the tensions expressed by non-White NYC teachers concerning the teaching of writing. She talked about writing skills dilemmas being embedded in the way race, class, and language get played out in the classroom and the neighborhood community. These were issues that I had not previously heard discussed so openly at a writing project session.

This, for me, monumental meeting of teacher representatives from these two projects was provocative, inspiring, and paved the way for a larger meeting that followed at the University of Pennsylvania under the leadership of Susan Lytle and the Philadelphia Writing Project, where concrete steps were made in the formation of the Urban Sites Network within NWP. At this gathering of urban teachers and teacher-consultants from around the country, folks were talking, testifying, and testing strategies to better meet the writing needs of their specific student populations. I remember African American teacher Deborah Jumpp (Philadelphia Writing Project) and Millie Veal (BWP) rising as leaders, along with others, and finding their way to the national forefront. This was my first experience with a substantial number of Black writing project teachers on the national level. Change had begun.

To walk into our annual NWP meeting today, one would notice a stark difference from my 1981 experience. The room is more colorful now, with languages and idioms other than English being spoken in conversations among and between teachers and teacher-consultants as well as university and college professors. Indeed, we have come a long way since the early days.

On both the national and my local site levels, we have come closer to actualizing bell hooks's definition of "critical consciousness"—a place where one feels recognized and included. We have been transformed and must continue to be transformed. Is there a place for lifting every voice in a writing project? Yes, there is—through constant, deliberate reflection and conscious action within each individual site.

Proselytizing the Project

IN THE EARLY YEARS OF THE NATIONAL WRITING PROJECT, we invited potential new site directors to come to Berkeley to visit with the staff and to observe and participate in a BAWP invitational summer institute—an incomparable experience for those who were able to do it. When visitors observed teacher demonstrations and sat in on writing groups, the model became clear to them. These visits to BAWP helped many new sites get off to a strong start.

We were also visited by a number of people during those early years who were not directly tied to the project. One such visit helped us understand that we had a ways to go before every teacher in America understood the essential importance of writing education. A group of teachers from out of state called and requested a meeting to learn how we dealt with writing. On the scheduled morning, after the group of six or so were comfortably in their circle of chairs, Keith Caldwell began talking to them about the writing project. Keith has a humorous but deadpan manner that he plays to advantage with most every group he works with, but on this day, he could tell that something was very seriously wrong. The teachers looked totally puzzled. Finally, one woman slowly raised her hand and asked, "Isn't this a handwriting project?"

But most people who contacted us were under no such misapprehension. For directors of new sites who were unable to come to Berkeley, we began to hold two-to three-day planning meetings at their sites. I loved these meetings. I got to know areas of the country I probably would never have seen otherwise. I loved these meetings also because I could say so much more about the writing project when I talked directly to the new directors than I could have ever put into words in an article or on an application form. We worked from morning to evening, and with each different planning meeting, I took directors through a full year in the life of a writing project, telling as many stories as I could to make my points. I spoke about the problems we'd had as well as the successes. I wove in what we were now learning from other sites—such as the daily log idea from Les Whipp, director of the Nebraska project, and the detailed chart of teacher roles and responsibilities that Don Gallehr had devised for his almost totally teacher-directed project, the initial Boot Camps at the Northern California Writing Project. At the Boot Camps, teachers camped out together for two days and nights prior to the summer institute. We did our best to make these planning meetings as valuable as trips to Berkeley would have been.

One visit in particular stands out for me. I was planning to visit with the Wiregrass Writing Project in Troy, Alabama, but before I left, Richard Graves from the Sun Belt Writing Project, also in Alabama, called to ask if I would also be willing to stop in Jacksonville to meet with a group of key people interested in the NWP, and of course I agreed. Betsy Dismukes, director of the Wiregrass Writing Project at the time, drove me to Jacksonville. When we pulled up to my hotel and saw on the marquee "Welcome National Writing Project," I realized this meeting might be more than I had planned on. At dinner that evening I discovered that I was going to be the keynote speaker to kick off a day-long conference honoring a group of Alabama writing project teachers. The next morning when I stood behind the podium, I faced a large auditorium filled with teachers, university faculty, school and district administrators, and members of the Alabama State Department of Education. This was the "group of key people" I had been asked to meet. I didn't have enough time to get nervous. My talk went smoothly—much better than usual. I had always thought I was better speaking to a small group than a large audience. Even though I knew the writing project as well as I knew my own face, this was the first time I had to give such a talk without the time to plan it and jot down the three or four pages of notes I usually thought I needed. This time it was spontaneous, just as it was when I spoke to directors in the planning sessions. It was a wonderful and freeing moment for me, for it was the first hint I had that I spoke much better to a large group, on this subject at least, if I just looked out at them and started talking. (A few years later, after I had given another well-received, spontaneous talk to a large audience of Iowa teachers, a teacher stopped me in the lobby to tell me that I had broken every one of the rules of public speaking.)

Exploring BAWP: An Early Visit to the Summer Institute

In the early days of the project, we had many visitors to Berkeley interested in initiating their own versions of the Bay Area Writing Project. Here, Don Gallehr, longtime director of the Northern Virginia Writing Project, writes of his first BAWP visit.

One of the statements in the proposal guidelines was, "The basic structure of BAWP is simple and easily replicated, and its assumptions and principles easily adopted." I would add to this the phrase "once seen," because seeing the BAWP Summer Institute and directors in action helped me enormously. We saw a teacher demonstration. We saw poet-participant Josephine Miles lead a workshop. We saw James Moffett, one of the nation's major voices in writing education, with his leg in a cast, quietly observing the institute from a seat in the back of the room. We saw fellows gathered on the Berkeley campus's lush lawns under shade trees in reading/writing groups. In their offices, we met the project secretaries and talked to Jim Gray and Miles Myers, then administrative director of BAWP. Up to that point, it was the most exciting two days of my career.

The most important image for me during our visit was watching Jim and Miles hold a private conversation, standing outside while the fellows nearby bought sandwiches from lunch carts. A simple act, two leaders conferring, one associated with the university, the other with the schools. Their stance and manner of conversation showed me, even from a distance, the respect they had for each other and the commitment they had for the project. Over the years, I have had similar conversations with my project colleagues from the schools, and I can trace the respect I have for them to this conversation I watched between Jim and Miles.

⌒ *The Bumpy Road to National Funding* ⌒

IN SPITE OF OUR NUMEROUS FUNDING SOURCES, we had a constant need for more money, and it seemed we were always on the edge of a precipice. At times I felt I heard the whispers in D. H. Lawrence's story "The Rocking Horse Winner": "We must have more money, we must have more money." The project kept growing, and we were writing new grant proposals and new amendments during the first three years of NEH funding just to keep up with the demand. There was a constant push to meet deadlines, and once we had to put Miles's administrative assistant, Cathy Hill, on a red-eye special to Washington, D.C., to meet the next day's NEH deadline.

My brother-in-law turned it into a joke. Every year he'd ask the same question, "How's it going this year?" And every year he'd listen to me moan that the end was near, and then, later in the year, he'd ask again, and I'd tell him we had been saved. As scary as it was, we never crashed because we did get a lot of grants. The Carnegie Corporation of New York supported us for six years after Michael Scriven had completed his evaluation. The National Endowment for the Humanities supported us for eleven years with grants and amendments, far beyond its preferred three-year limit. John Hale, who replaced Bill Russell as our program officer, once told me about the inevitable yearly scenario at the NEH's annual meeting to set grant policy. The chairperson would state the agreed upon policy that NEH awards would run for three years and three years only. The chairperson would then ask the staff, "Are we agreed upon this?" And the staff would then nod yes. But then someone would raise a hand and ask, "Does this mean that we won't be able to give any more grants to the New York Public Library?" Someone else would say, "What about the National Writing Project?" And policy reform would be put off for another year. But when the endowment just couldn't fund us any longer, Bill Bennett, the chair of NEH, called the Andrew Mellon Foundation and urged his friends at Mellon to pick up the funding for this worthy project. I received a call from Richard Ekman at NEH telling me that nothing like this had ever happened before. The Andrew Mellon Foundation funded us for nine more years, and by the end of that time, the National Writing Project was funded by the United States Congress.

⌒

RECRUITING DIVERSITY

I have always believed that the parts of the writing project model fit together like the workings of a quality watch. That is not to say there have not been glitches. For one, we depend on the talented teachers who become our TCs to recommend other talented teachers for the Invitational Summer Institute. Naturally enough, these teachers feel most comfortable recommending teachers they know well, who are also, quite possibly, teachers they work with. Thus, while it is our intention to cast a broad net, we can very easily find ourselves fishing from a restricted pool. This is the problem that Bay Area Writing Project director Carol Tateishi decided to confront head-on almost a decade ago. Here she tells the story.

The Bay Area Writing Project has, since the beginning, been committed to diversity. We knew that if we were going to make real changes in writing education in our part of California, we would need a summer institute that mirrored ethnically and geographically the teaching population of the Bay Area, including the core cities, the bordering working-class communities, and the upper-middle-class suburbs beyond. But that wasn't happening. Despite what we thought were our best efforts, a disproportionate number of our summer fellows were white teachers from the more privileged communities.

In 1992, we decided to make a concerted effort to turn our words into action. Our priority would be increasing our diversity.

We began where we had always begun in our search for talented nominees, with our BAWP teacher-consultants. But this time we made clear our concern that if BAWP was to remain relevant to the teachers of the Bay Area, we needed the participation of more teachers of color. We made phone calls to TCs who we thought might be particularly able to help us in our quest.

We also used a technique called "cloud seeding." This meant getting the word out in every way short of tacking notices on telephone polls. I presented at district principals' meetings in Oakland and San Francisco, followed up those meetings with calls to interested administrators, visited target schools to speak to teachers about BAWP programs, and made calls to educators we knew shared our goals.

At the same time, we realized that we should work on making our other summer programs—those that we sponsor in addition to the invitational summer institute—more accessible to a larger range of teachers. We found new ways to work with the university to restructure course fees. We also expanded our programs to include short summer courses to accommodate teachers who needed to teach summer school or were in year-round schools, and we successfully pushed to get district Title I funds to pay teachers to attend our programs.

We began to make headway in our effort to involve more African American teachers in our programs, and we made a number of inroads into new schools, particularly in Oakland, but we were still pretty unconnected to schools with large numbers of bilingual and English-language learners.

However, I had an idea. A few years earlier, California Tomorrow, an organization whose work I have always admired, published a work—*Crossing the School House Border*—which featured teachers who were making a difference in highly diverse classrooms. I called Moyra Contraras and Judy Bebelaar, two BAWP TCs profiled in the book, to check out other featured teachers particularly strong in the field of bilingual teaching. Armed with their recommendations, I made cold calls to this handful of teachers I didn't even know. Looking back now, I wonder at myself, explaining to these teachers why I was calling and asking them to apply to the BAWP Invitational Summer Institute, without their even knowing if they would be accepted and, in most cases, knowing very little about BAWP other than its name.

One of these calls, however, paid off big. That was the call to Winnie Porter, a Latina who had immigrated to the United States when she was about four. Winnie was a K–2 Spanish bilingual teacher at Cesar Chavez Elementary School in San Francisco's Mission District. Winnie seemed unfazed by my unexpected call, and she was interested in BAWP. However, in addition to teaching, Winnie was a leader in the National Education Association, and because of this role, every summer she had responsibilities in Washington, D.C. But I persevered for the next few years, and finally Winnie had a summer free, came to the institute, and immediately afterward began nominating other teachers from her school. Three came. Eventually, even the principal came. This group has been a wellspring of an ongoing stream of new summer fellows. They have helped make possible a number of new BAWP programs that are dependent on the leadership of bilingual and ESL teachers.

Looking back at our efforts to build a more representative writing project, I'm aware that we put to work several techniques more associated with selling home improvements than with drawing distinguished teachers into a highly regarded professional development program. We asked our TCs to provide us with leads, we engaged in cloud seeding to get the word of our product out through every possible avenue, we provided economically attractive deals, we made cold calls to likely prospects, and we depended on the word of mouth of our satisfied customers.

This proactive work has made a huge difference. Our bench is now deep with teacher-consultants and friends in the Bay Area education community who are part of our diversity building effort. Our programs are designed to attract to the institute teachers who may have been invisible otherwise, and our numerous partnerships with schools in low-income communities are a rich source of new knowledge and the mentoring of new teachers.

Through all this, our goal has remained the same: to address issues of equity in Bay Area schools by increasing our project's capacity to improve the teaching and learning of writing in the diverse classrooms of the Bay Area.

~

One day in 1988, I was called into Assistant Vice President Alice Cox's office at the University of California Office of the President and informed that I had to relinquish one of my two California directorships—either director of the Bay Area Writing Project or director of the California Writing Project. The rationale for this decision was that as director of the California Writing Project I was in a potential conflict of interest as the administrator of funds awarded to the Bay Area Writing Project. I was stunned. I felt I was being penalized for being successful.

Because the local, state, and national projects were interrelated like a set of Russian babushka dolls, it had never seemed to me that I had three different jobs. I believed it was important that a single executive director have active oversight over the total network. The Bay Area Writing Project was the lead agency and center of the National Writing Project, and it was the one project that kept me in constant touch with classroom teachers. But if I gave up the California Writing Project, I would be cut off from nineteen of the National Writing Project's strongest and most productive sites and from the statewide network that was the model for similar networks in other states.

I turned the Bay Area Writing Project over to Mary Ann Smith, its brilliant codirector, who knew the writing project model as well as I did. If I had to make a choice between BAWP and CWP, I might as well give up the project that had the heaviest load and took up most of my time.

When I retired from UC Berkeley in 1991, I continued on as director of the National Writing Project until January 1994, when Richard Sterling, then director of the New York City Writing Project, was elected by the NWP Board of Directors as executive director of the National Writing Project. With this major change, Mary Ann became director of the California Writing Project, and Carol Tateishi became director of the Bay Area Writing Project.

These three new leaders have had no difficulty maintaining the interrelation of these key units of the writing project. The project at the local, state, and national levels has thrived because it is not about a person; it is about an idea. And because the project has always created an atmosphere in which teachers take charge of their professional lives, when I departed there was no shortage of gifted leaders available to advance that idea.

When the National Writing Project Board of Directors chose Richard Sterling as my replacement, they could not have made a wiser decision. Richard, who had extensive experience with the National Writing Project as director of the New York City Writing Project, was eager to get started, and that enthusiasm has only continued to grow.

He came to the job with many goals, and most of them have by now been realized many times over. We are a far more visible participant in the school reform movement. Under Richard's leadership, the National Writing Project has grown to 168 sites in forty-nine states and Puerto Rico. Federal funding is now three times what it was. Networking—site to site and teacher to teacher—has increased enormously. A sophisticated project-to-project, Web-based communication system for directors and teacher consultants is in place. There are far more professional opportunities for teacher leaders at writing project sites throughout the nation. And, finally, both the teachers in the writing project and the students they work with are much more representative of the diverse American community the project serves.

All this has evolved from the strength of a simple, powerful idea, which, like many groundbreaking ideas, wasn't as obvious at the time of its origin as it is now in retrospect. I did not in the beginning truly understand the power of teachers teaching teachers. It took me decades of work as a high school teacher, as a trainer of student teachers, as a participant in numerous professional development programs, to discover and embrace the revolutionary notion that classroom teachers are best qualified to teach other teachers.

As dedicated as I became to the teachers-teaching-teachers model, it took a team of people to turn this originally hazy notion into a successful national model. I will be forever grateful to those who worked with me in those early years: to Rod Park, who provided the university support we needed, and especially to fellow teachers Cap Lavin, Miles Myers, Mary K. Healy, and Keith Caldwell, among others.

In the beginning, we asked ourselves, Could teachers of different grade levels be brought together successfully? It took us one year to realize they could. Could a carefully selected group of strong teachers work together all day for five weeks each summer? They not only could, they relished the experience. Could they go into other schools and conduct successful three-hour workshops? We found many who could, and we helped others prepare during our monthly Saturday conferences. Could teachers of writing, many of whom were hesitant to write themselves, use editing/response groups to hone their craft and build their confidence? We have seen thousands of teachers of writing do just that, and who now proudly call themselves writers.

With its expanding influence as a voice for school reform and with the continuing growth of both the number of sites and the quantity and quality of its programs, the National Writing Project has met what evaluator Paul Diederich in our earliest years called the "test of the market."

Yet, our message of teachers at the center still needs to be spread. Carol Tateishi tells of attending, a few years ago, an invitational meeting of a professional group concerned with school standards. This was a large and varied assembly, but one with classroom teachers in the distinct minority. Carol listened for several days to a discussion she believed was giving short shrift to the concerns of teachers, and finally she stood to ask a question: "Don't you know that what is being planned here must have the support of our best teachers or it is going nowhere?"

I believe Carol's words on this occasion provide the best yardstick for judging the success of school reform efforts. Well-intended mandates that ignore the voices of classroom teachers will fail. Programs that emerge from the collective wisdom of those who work most closely with our children have, as the National Writing Project has demonstrated, an odds-on chance at success.

Basic Components of the NWP Staff Development Model and Program Design

~ Project Administration ~

- With rare exception, all NWP projects are located on university and college campuses.

- Site directors, with some exceptions, are typically professors of English or English education, and codirectors, typically, are classroom teachers.

- Most sites are assisted by advisory committees, steering committees, or councils.

- Local sites are usually funded by multiple sources that include host campus and surrounding school district support and, at some sites, additional extramural support.

~ The Invitational Summer Institute ~

SCHEDULE, STIPENDS, AND CREDIT

- The summer institute usually runs for five weeks, all day, four days a week, with a three-day weekend for writing, reading, and preparation.

- Participants, whenever possible, receive modest stipends to cover expenses of tuition, fees, books, and incidentals.

- Teachers usually receive graduate credit for participating in the institute.

SELECTION OF PARTICIPANTS

- Careful selection, e.g., some process that includes nomination, application, and interview, is central to this teachers-teaching-teachers project.

- Teachers are selected on the basis of their demonstrable success as teachers of writing and for their promise as equally successful teachers of other teachers.

- Directors seek teachers who are both strong and open.

- Participants are drawn from all grade levels, K–university, and from across the curriculum, as well as from English and language arts.

- Participants are drawn from both public and private schools in urban, suburban, and rural areas.

- Many NWP sites regularly seek out interested school administrators and other policy-makers as full-time summer participants.

- The local National Writing Project site director has final authority in selection of summer institute participants.

PRE-INSTITUTE SPRING MEETING

For the participants, this initial spring meeting sets a supportive and collegial tone, calms pre-institute jitters, and provides an opportunity to meet everyone involved in the summer institute. For the project staff, the spring meeting is an opportunity to give reading and writing assignments, explain details of the summer schedule, and describe the participant demonstrations of good teaching practice. In short, this important meeting does much to guarantee a strong start to the summer institute.

TEACHER DEMONSTRATIONS

The basic writing project model is quite simple. Effective teachers in the schools can be identified and brought together in summer institutes, where they are trained to teach other teachers. This teachers–teaching–teachers idea is the heart of the project. Classroom teachers are believable as no other consultants can ever be. They have a knowledge about effective teaching based on their own experience in real classrooms that no other consultant outside of the classroom can ever match. And teachers have responded to this model of inservice education in great numbers. This model has its beginnings in the teacher demonstrations of the summer institute.

- These "trial-run" workshops, a key component of the summer institute, provide an opportunity for successful teachers of writing to demonstrate a range of effective approaches and to prepare for school-year inservice demonstrations.

- The teacher demonstrations tap that knowledge about writing and the teaching of writing that comes from the classroom practice of effective teachers. That knowledge is as important to the writing project as the knowledge that comes from research. It is also the knowledge that practicing teachers find most credible.

- Since teachers need adequate presentation time for effective teaching demonstrations, the institute schedule should reflect the importance of this key component. For example, at some sites each of the twenty-five participants has one and a half hours for his/her teaching demonstration.

- The most successful teacher demonstrations communicate not only what the teacher does but also why the teacher thinks this particular practice works. The emphasis upon the *why* as well as the *what* is important: it provides a theoretical underpinning and it accents a considered approach to writing beyond mere gimmickry.

- Because teaching other teachers is a new experience for most summer participants, calling for a new set of skills, the participants profit by coaching prior to their first teaching demonstration. This coaching, typically a one-on-one session with the director, codirector, or a former participant, is a walkthrough of the planned demonstration—an opportunity to check for focus, efficient use of time, opportunities for group involvement, and so on.

- Summer participants, as future NWP teacher-consultants, will also profit by feedback from their peers and from the project staff following their first trial-run demonstration.

WRITING AND EDITING/RESPONSE GROUPS

So much attention has been given to the fact that teachers do a great deal of writing in the summer institutes and school-year workshops that the project is frequently referred to as a "writers' project." More than anything else the project does, its insistence that teachers of writing must write has caught the interest and imagination of the larger community. Writing is the ultimate hands-on experience for the National Writing Project.

- That teachers of writing must write, as well as read and talk about the teaching of writing, is one of the major assumptions of the writing project, important not only in the invitational summer institute but also in the range of follow-up programs sponsored by the project.

- The summer institute gives teachers the rare opportunity of coming together as a community of writers over a sustained period of time, freed from the demands of teaching, to write and to share their pieces with other teachers of writing in regularly scheduled editing/response groups. This experience is central to the development of a teacher of writing and central to the training of an NWP teacher-consultant.

- Writing and presenting drafts to peer response groups for comment, reaction, and editorial assistance and then revising the initial drafts allow teachers to experience what they ask or should ask of their own students.

- That teachers of writing begin to write in NWP programs is important; that so many of these teachers become writers of such exceptional pieces is the unexpected surprise.

- Most NWP sites publish anthologies of teachers' summer writings.

- The time necessary for editing/response groups—two or three full afternoons each week—cannot be compromised by other demands upon the schedule.

- The continuation of editing/response groups after the close of the summer institute is encouraged—though little encouragement is needed. Some groups have continued throughout the lifetime of particular NWP sites.

READINGS AND RESEARCH

- An initial and continuing goal of the writing project is to disseminate to classroom teachers the best that is known about writing and the teaching of writing from practice and from research. Therefore, it is the responsibility of the summer institute, in addition to tapping the best practices of exemplary teachers, to introduce teachers to the growing body of research and literature in the field and to a larger professional community.

- While it is difficult during the five-week summer institute for teachers to read everything worthwhile in the field of written composition, the institute starts a process of professional reading that can, in turn, continue throughout a teacher's career and in all ongoing project programs.

- The National Writing Project, by honoring both research and practice, can break down the wall that has long separated the world of teaching from the world of research.

- The National Writing Project also promotes teacher research:

  - Teacher research opens yet another door to the professional development of the classroom teacher.

  - Teacher research, as research, can contribute to the general body of knowledge about the teaching of writing.

  - Teachers engaged in teacher research report growth in their own teaching effectiveness and increased authority in their roles as NWP teacher-consultants.

  - Teacher research, possibly more than any other writing project activity, increases teacher interest in research and promotes the dissemination of research findings.

PLANNING THE SUMMER INSTITUTE SCHEDULE

- The summer institute should be balanced in its key components—teacher demonstrations, writing and editing/response groups, reading, and research—and should protect the time required for each against the many other competing claims upon the institute schedule.

- The summer institute should provide an opportunity for participants to make connections between all of the key components.

Follow-up Programs

Unlike many programs that have preceded it, the writing project does not come to a close once its summer program is over. Teachers are kept together over time through a range of focused and systematic programs and through their new roles as writing project teacher-consultants, the teachers who teach teachers in the workshops conducted at school sites throughout the school year. The National Writing Project recognizes that a classroom teacher's education is never complete and therefore provides a carefully planned and coherent continuing education program for practicing classroom teachers.

CONTINUITY PROGRAMS

- The network of National Writing Project sites offers participants in the invitational summer institutes a range of programs for continued training and support. Typical of such continuity programs are the following: monthly Saturday meetings; advanced summer institutes; teacher research programs; ongoing editing/response groups; councils; target programs for summer fellows with common interests (writing across the curriculum, writing in the primary grades, etc.); opportunities to plan and participate in local, regional, and state conferences; university seminar series, and so on.

- The National Writing Project offers opportunities for increased professional responsibility through leadership roles within the project, including paid teacher-consultant opportunities, paid inservice coordinator positions, membership on advisory and steering committees, and writing project staff positions (full-time, part-time, and voluntary).

- The NWP offers regular regional and national meetings for the support and the interaction of site directors and codirectors.

- Directors and teacher-consultants can serve the project as NWP regional directors or NWP advisory board members.

- *The Quarterly*, the NWP journal, provides directors and teacher-consultants with publishing opportunities.

INSERVICE PROGRAMS

- While the invitational summer institute offers classroom teachers the most intense writing project experience, the project has its greatest impact on the greatest number of teachers through its inservice programs in the schools.

- While there is clear justification for certain single-session workshops, e.g., a follow-up session to a completed series or a preview session to planned series programs, it is the National Writing Project's policy to offer inservice workshops in series and not as single sessions.

- The typical NWP workshop series is voluntary, ten sessions in length, with each session lasting three hours. There are, however, alternatives at various sites across the country that are also preferable to the single-shot session: an intensive three-day, all-day inservice program at a school or district site; a five-session series of three-hour workshops; a series of one-on-one coaching sessions with selected classroom teachers; released-time programs at selected schools, etc.

- The typical NWP inservice series will have one experienced teacher-consultant serving as coordinator. The coordinator's role is varied and includes items such as the following:
  - Assisting project staff in planning the total series, including selecting the teacher-consultant staff
  - Introducing the project teacher-consultants at the different workshop sessions
  - Maintaining continuity throughout the series
  - Assigning and responding to teachers' writings, learning logs, etc.
  - Completing a final report for project staff
- The NWP inservice coordinator is a paid position, with stipends varying from site to site.
- NWP inservice programs are partnership programs, designed to serve school and district needs. Pre-series planning meetings are always advisable and frequently necessary.
- NWP summer institute participants do not serve as writing project teacher-consultants until they're ready to offer effective workshops in the schools. The local project will offer opportunities to project teachers to develop and practice inservice presentations. Some teachers, though they may serve in other ways, may never be ready for this particular project responsibility.

ᕈ *Evaluation* ᕈ

- Each National Writing Project site conducts some annual evaluation of project impact.
- Informal, written teacher responses to summer institutes and to school-year inservice programs prove an excellent source of recommendation for continual project improvement and refinement.

- Site directors and teachers are encouraged to use multiple modes when assessing project impact on improved student writing: holistic pre- and post-evaluation, portfolio assessment, case studies, and ethnographic studies, etc.

- Networks of NWP sites supported by state funds should allocate some portion of state funding for project evaluation.

- The NWP lead agency has published *Profiles of the National Writing Project* and will revise this publication as new evaluation studies are completed.

James Gray enjoyed a distinguished career as an English teacher and teacher-educator before he launched the Bay Area Writing Project in 1974. For the next twenty years, he worked to advance the writing project model, which now flourishes at 168 NWP sites at colleges and universities in 49 states. Gray retired as the NWP executive director in 1994, but remains active as a member of the NWP's board of directors.